W. Naismith

Naismith's Hand-Book of Hamilton and Neighbourhood

W. Naismith

Naismith's Hand-Book of Hamilton and Neighbourhood

ISBN/EAN: 9783337372286

Printed in Europe, USA, Canada, Australia, Japan

Cover: Foto ©Thomas Meinert / pixelio.de

More available books at **www.hansebooks.com**

Naismith's

Hand-Book

OF

HAMILTON

And Neighbourhood.

HAMILTON:

W. NAISMITH, 38 CADZOW STREET.

GLASGOW: J. MENZIES & CO.

HANDBOOK

OF

HAMILTON.

CONTENTS.

HANDBOOK.

W E purpose to sketch the early history, notable events and associations, and present condition and prospects of Hamilton and vicinage. The ancient designation of the parish was Cadzow, the etymology of which is uncertain; and the present name was assumed by virtue of a charter, of date 3d July, 1445, granted by James II. of Scotland to James, first Lord Hamilton. In the hoary ruins which crown the precipitous banks of Avon, the leading street of the town, and numerous familiar objects, the ancient name still finds preservation. The parish of Hamilton from north to south is six miles in length, and of nearly equal breadth from east to west, the extent in square miles being 22·25, and in acres 14,240. The northern boundary is formed by the parish of Bothwell; on the east are Dalziel, Cambusnethan, Dalserf, and Stonehouse; on the south and south-west the parish of Glassford; and on the west Blantyre. The district is rich in mineral wealth and natural beauty. The Clyde and Avon waters its broad smiling plains, whose fertility and advanced cultivation have long made the locality in reality as well as in name—the orchard of Scotland; while, as the cradle of a powerful race, which exerted a momentous influence on national events, and as the occasional theatre of great occurrences, history has accorded to it in the past a prominent place. For the

2

future, the eminence to be attained will be industrial and commercial, the opening up of its coal field, destined to be second in importance to none in Scotland, having changed, and being likely in a way scarcely possible to realise still further to change, the character of the district.

LEGENDARY.

The ancient kingdom of Strathclyde embraced Lanarkshire within its bounds. After the withdrawal of the Roman power, it is certain that the inhabitants, the Romanised Britains, if they had ever been Christianised, lapsed into heathenism. The received local apostle was St Kentigern, otherwise known as St Mungo, a contemporary of Columba, and regarding three of whose renowned miracles the armorial bearings of the city of Glasgow are a perpetuation. Kentigern had a controversy with a Strathclyde King Morken, and in a sort of despair left to do duty among the Southern Britains in Wales. There afterwards, however, occupied the throne of Strathclyde, Rederech, a pious monarch, eager to restore the gospel to his benighted subjects, and at his desire Kentigern returned. Rederech had his castle at Cadzow, near Barncluith Burn, where Castlehill House now stands. Of him it is related that he had invited a stranger to hunt with him at Cadzow, who, during the intervals of the chase, made himself so agreeable to the fair Queen that she gave him a ring she had received from her husband, and otherwise showed a degree of favour to him, which, on its discovery, enraged Rederech. In a fit of furious jealousy he possessed himself of the ring while the knight was sleeping, threw it into the river, and then, sending for the Queen, asked her for it, and threatened death if it was not produced. The trembling lady sent to the stranger for the ring, but, of course, it was not forthcoming, and, as a last resource, a message was sent to Glasgow to St Mungo, imploring his assistance. The good man was sorry for the Queen, and sent one of his servants to fish, and on opening the mouth of the first fish caught, the ring was found. St Mungo sent it to the Queen, she hastened with it to the King, and her life was spared. This legend is taken from the Breviary of Aberdeen and other sources, and a representation of it forms the reverse of Bishop Wishart of Glasgow's seal in the 13th century. Strathclyde had less renown from its political history than as the theatre of the triumphs of St Kentigern, and it is through him that Rederech comes out of the utter darkness political into the doubtful light of ecclesiastical history.

DAVID I. AT CADZOW.

To step at once from the uncertain footing of the sixth to the increasingly strengthening ground of the twelfth and thirteenth centuries, we find the old Scottish kings in 1153 and 1289 holding their courts at Cadzow, which continued to be royal property till after the Battle of Bannockburn. David I., of saintly memory, before coming to the Throne, by his brother Edgar's dying request, was created Lord of Cumbria, in which district Cadzow was included. He found this portion of his heritage in a miserable state, and sought to ameliorate the condition of his people by the establishment of civil laws and the restoration of ecclesiastical jurisdiction. He granted the Church of Cadzow as an endowment to the newly-founded Cathedral of Glasgow; and, uniting a taste for gardening and love of sport with religious fervour, many of the oaks at Cadzow

are believed to have been planted by the kingly hand,
and here he hunted

> "The mightiest of all the beasts of chase
> That roam in woody Caledon!"

From here, also, Royal charters were dated : *Apud
Castrum de Cadichow*—at our Castle of Cadzow.

CIVIL AND RELIGIOUS STRUGGLES.

The events of which the district was subsequently the
scene are well known in Scottish history. In November,
1650, Cromwell sent General Lambert and Commissary-
General Whalley to Hamilton, with five regiments of
cavalry, to overawe the west country Covenanters or
to bring them over to· his own terms. They were
attacked by Colonel Kerr with 1500 horsemen from
Ayrshire. The Covenanters succeeded in securing a
number of the horses ; but Lambert having rallied
his forces, overtook the " spoil-encumbered foe " two
miles west of Hamilton, killed Colonel Kerr and
about 100 of his troops, and took many prisoners.

On Sunday, 1st June, 1679, Captain Graham (afterwards Viscount Dundee) on his way to the field of
Drumclog, seized, near Hamilton, John King, a field
preacher, and seventeen other people, whom he bound
in pairs, and drove before him towards Loudon Hill.
Mr King, who was probably in disguise, is described
by Crighton as a " bra muckle carl with a white hat
and a great bob of ribbons on the back o't."   The
Covenanters after their success at Drumclog, deeming
it unlawful to fight on the Sabbath except in self-
defence, returned to the field of action, where they
offered up thanks to the Almighty for the victory they
had gained ; after which they took some refreshment
in Strathaven, and marched to Hamilton in the
evening. Next day (June 2) flushed with victory,

they resolved to make an attack on Glasgow. One division of them, commanded by Mr Hamilton, attempted to penetrate by Gallowgate, and another party entered by the High Street. But Lord Ross had so completely barricaded the streets, and made such a resistance that the Covenanters were soon compelled to retire, with the loss of Walter Paterson of Carbarns, and five of their party killed and several wounded. After their repulse at Glasgow they rallied on Tollcross Muir, and returned to Hamilton. The more moderate party (June 20) drew up a paper which afterwards obtained the name of the "Hamilton declaration." The purport of it was to forbear all angry disputes and mutual recriminations for the present, to disclaim any intention to overturn the Government, civil or ecclesiastical, and to refer all matters of importance to a free Parliament and a lawfully chosen General Assembly. This proposal was, of course, rejected by the violent party. Their guard was attacked in the night-time at Hamilton Ford, and one of their number (James Cleland) killed. On Saturday, 21st June, the royal army, under the Duke of Monmouth, about 500 strong, reached Bothwell Muir within two miles of the Covenanters' camp. On the morning of Sunday 22d June, the Covenanters, amounting to about 4000 men, were posted between the Clyde and the town of Hamilton, on the brow of the brae near Bothwell Bridge. Rathillet, Hall, and Turnbull, with three troops under their command, and one piece of brass ordnance, guarded the important pass. The result of this most unfortunate rencounter is well known. The Covenanters were put to flight. They fled with great loss chiefly in the direction of Glassford and Strathaven. Gordon of Earlston had reached the parish of Hamilton with a party of Galloway men,

when they met their discomfited brethren at Allows-
hill, near Quarter, where Gordon was met and killed.
A great number of the Covenanters found shelter in
Hamilton woods, and the amiable Duchess Anne,
requesting that the soldiers might not be permitted
to enter her plantations, Monmouth instantly gave
orders to that effect. About 1200 men were taken
prisoners on the spot.

NOTABLE EVENTS.

The Hamiltons were great opposers of the Union.
In 1707, when that event took place, 500 troops
assembled at Hamilton to resist it by force of arms.
It was expected that 7000 or 8000 would have met ;
but the Duke of Hamilton disapproved of the
measure.

On the death of the Duke of Douglas in 1761, the
house of Hamilton, as male representatives of the
Douglases, laid claim to the estates, under a per-
suasion that Mr Douglas, son and heir of Lady Jane
Stewart, sister of the Duke of Douglas was a supposi-
tious child taken at Paris from the real parents. A
long lawsuit was the result. It was decided in Paris
and in the Court of Session in favour of the
Hamiltons ; but, on an appeal to the House of Peers,
was ultimately decided in favour of Mr Douglas,
afterwards created Lord Douglas—the Duke of
Hamilton retaining the titles.

In 1777, Douglas, Duke of Hamilton, coming of
age, raised in Hamilton, for the service of the country,
the 82d Regiment of Foot, which afterwards highly
distinguished itself in the American War.

On 11th June, 1782, the Duke of Hamilton, as
Duke of Brandon in England, was called to take his
seat in the House of Lords as a British peer. This

paved the way to all the Scottish nobility who have since obtained similar honours and privileges.

The parish has been the birthplace and occasional residence of many eminent characters. The celebrated Dr Cullen, sometimes represented as born at Lanark in 1712, appears distinctly from the session-books of Hamilton to have been born two years later in the parish of Hamilton. Dr Cullen was magistrate of Hamilton for several years. The celebrated Lord Cochrane spent many of his early days in the parish. The father of the late Professor Millar of Glasgow was parochial clergyman ; as was also the father of the late Dr Baillie of London, and of his celebrated sister, Joanna Baillie. Principal Cunningham, the theologian, was baptised in Muir Street Secession Church on 2d October, 1805 ; and Dr Livingstone, the African traveller, was a reader in the library of the same congregation.

ANTIQUITIES.

The Castle of Cadzow is the most prominent antiquity in the parish. It stands in Hamilton wood, amidst the softest and most picturesque of sylvan surroundings, on the summit of a precipitous rock, the base of which is washed by the Avon. Who its founders were is unknown, although it is surmised that Caw or Cay was the first of the royal race who took up their residence in this quarter. The Castle continued in the possession of the Crown until it was granted by Robert the Bruce to Sir Walter Fitz-Gilbert. With only two short interruptions, it has ever since continued in the hands of his descendants. The first of these interruptions was about the year 1581, when it fell for a short time into the hands of Captain Stewart. The other suspension, equally short in duration, was in 1654, when by Cromwell's act of grace and pardon,

William Duke of Hamilton deceased, was exempted
from all benefit thereof, and his estates forfeited, there
being reserved out of them £400 per annum to his
Duchess during her life, and after her death to each
of his four daughters and their heirs for ever. The
Castle of Cadzow seems to have been repaired at
different times. The keep, with the fosse around it,
a narrow bridge on the south over the fosse, and a
well inside, are still in good preservation, and are all
of polished stone of a reddish colour. Several vaults
and the walls, probably of the chapel, are still visible.
Cadzow Castle is celebrated in Scott's fine ballad—

"When princely Hamilton's abode,
    Ennobled Cadzow's Gothic towers,
The song went round, the goblet flowed,
    And revel sped the laughing hours.

Then, thrilling to the harp's gay sound,
    So sweetly rung each vaulted wall,
And echoed light the dancer's bound,
    As mirth and music cheered the hall.

But Cadzow's towers, in ruins laid,
    And vaults by ivy mantled o'er,
Thrill to the music of the shade
    Or echo Evan's hoarser roar."

The Castle of Darngaber (*i. e.*, the "house between
the waters," or, as some have supposed, the "hiding
place of the goats,") in the S.E. side of the parish is
said to have been built by Thomas de Hamilton, son
of Sir John de Hamilton, Dominus de Cadzow. Its
ruins stand on a small knoll at the extremity of a
tongue of land where two rivulets meet. The founda-
tions only of this ancient fortress can now be traced.
They are entirely of flat shingly stones, without lime,
and seem never to have been subjected to a tool.
Small vaults have been discovered, which are not
arched, but drawn together as conduits sometimes are.

It is probable, therefore, that Thomas de Hamilton did not build, but only repaired this castle.

The most perfect, and indeed the only tumulus, properly speaking, in the parish is at Meikle Earnock, about two miles south of Hamilton. It is about 12 feet in diameter and 8 feet high—it was formerly much larger—and hollow at the top. When broken into, several urns were found containing the ashes of human bones, some of them accompanied by the tooth of a horse. There was no inscription seen, but some of the urns, which were all of baked earth, were plain, and others decorated with moulding, probably to distinguish the quality of the deceased.

In the haugh to the north of the Palace there is an ancient moathill or seat of justice. It is about 30 feet in diameter at the base, and about 15 or 16 feet high, and is flat at the top. When it stood formerly in the midst of the town, the hill formed part of the garden of an alehouse, and was dressed with the spade and adorned with plants. It cannot be less than eight or nine hundred years old, as no erections of the kind have been in use since the reign of Malcolm Canmore. Near the Moathill is an ancient stone cross about four feet high, bearing no inscription. It is said to have been the cross of the Netherton.

In the south of the parish a remarkable stone, about six feet high, but leaning considerably to one side, gives the immediate locality the name, "Crooked Stone." It is of freestone, and evidently very ancient. Mr Chalmers notices these bended stones as cromlechs of Druidical origin. A neighbouring farmer (says Mr William Patrick in his Statistical Account of Hamilton, written in 1847) lately set the stone upright, leaving posterity to wonder why it was called crooked stone.

The Barncluith gardens may be noticed amongst the antiquities of the district. The flower garden is cut out of the steep banks of Avon, two or three hundred feet high, and is divided into five terraces. These are flanked by terrace walls, covered with espaliers of various descriptions. The borders of the walls are crowded with a variety of evergreens cut into fantastic forms. In the centre of the great walk is a handsome pavilion fitted up with rustic chairs, and other curious pieces of furniture. The gardens and buildings have afforded infinite scope for the pencil of the artist and pen of the poet. They are believed to have been constructed by John Hamilton of Barncluith, commissary of Hamilton and Campsie, in 1583. He was son of Quinton Hamilton, who was killed fighting in the Queen's cause at the battle of Langside; and is reputed by tradition to have been deeply skilled in mathematics.

THE NOBLE FAMILY OF HAMILTON.

After the defeat of the English at Bannockburn the Barony of Cadzow changed hands for the last time, passing into the possession of the ancestors of its present owner. With the history of the Hamiltons, and their accession to wealth, honour, and dignities, the inhabitants were henceforth to be completely identified; and it may justly be said that wherever there appears a patriot, statesman, or warrior in the annals of the family, there also are found recorded proofs of the loyal support accorded them at every crisis by the "good men of the West," their retainers and dependants.

The English origin of the family is undoubted; how or when it took root north of the Tweed is not so clearly ascertained. Their lineage has been traced to Robert (Blanchmains) third Earl of Leicester, who

died 1190. Though it has not been proved, there is
nothing improbable in this descent; for the Earl's
second son was Bishop of St. Andrews, other relations figure in Scottish history of the period, and the
cinquefoil on a bloody shield, the heraldic bearing
from an early period of the Scottish Hamiltons, was
also that of the house of Leicester referred to. The
name, obviously territorial, is believed to have been
taken from some one of the numerous manors of
Hambleden, situated in Bucks and other English
counties. There is a legend connected with the origin
of the family, which, though fabulous, having been
quoted by Sir Archibald Alison, we do not apologise
for including in our narrative. Sir Gilbert de Hemelen,
Knight, was a warm admirer of the Bruce, and at the
English Court he ventured with chivalrous boldness
to give vent to his admiration. He was at once chal-
lenged by a parasite named de Spencer to mortal
combat. He slew his antagonist, and escaping to the
Scotch Court, met King Robert at Cadzow at the
head of a hunting party. As a modern minnie-singer
relates—

"Bold was the foremost hunter's look—majestic was his air;
Most firmly knit his head and limbs, and sable dark his hair."

After revealing himself to the Scotch King, and tell-
ing his story, he is embraced by the Bruce :—

"Enough, enough, Sir Gilbert, we give thee welcome here;
Look round thee, and where'er thine eye traverses far and near,
These acres broad shall be thine own, whilst thou that sword
  shall bring
To aid broad Scotland's cause and mine, for I am Bruce the
  King."

Subsequently the King bestows on the Knight the
hand of his niece, Isabel, in marriage. As connected
with this legend, it is explained that the family motto
"Through," and the crest with Oak and Saw arose

from Sir Gilbert taking in his flight the dress of a
wood-cutter and practising that primitive art, crying
to his servant "Through" to distract his attention
from his pursuers.

All legend to the contrary, the pedigree of the
family cannot be carried beyond (1) Walter Fitz-
Gilbert of Hamilton, who, in 1296 held lands in
Lanarkshire, and swore fealty to King Edward I. of
England as Overlord of Scotland, and in 1314 kept
the Castle of Bothwell for the English. His early
surrender of the fortress and of the English knights
and nobles who had fled to it from the field of Bannockburn, was rewarded by King Robert Bruce by
grants of the lands and baronies of Cadzow and
Machanshire, Kinneil, &c., lands forfeited by the
Cumyns and other adherents of England. He
attained the rank of knighthood, and married Mary,
daughter of Sir Adam of Gordon of Huntley, by
whom he left two sons. The elder (2) Sir David
Fitz-Walter Fitz-Gilbert was taken prisoner at the
battle of Neville's Cross, in 1346. He founded a
chantry in the Cathedral of Glasgow in 1361, and
appears among the barons in the Scottish Parliaments
in 1368, 1371, and 1373. His eldest son (3) Sir
David of Hamilton of Cadzow died before 1392, leaving by his wife, Janet of Keith, only daughter and
heiress of Sir William of Keith of Galston, five sons
and a daughter. The eldest son (4) Sir John of
Hamilton of Cadzow, married Janet, daughter of Sir
James of Douglas of Dalkeith, by whom he was the
father of (5) Sir James of Hamilton of Cadzow, who,
about 1422, married Janet, daughter of Alexander of
Livingston of Callander, by whom he had (6) Sir
James of Hamilton of Cadzow, and four other sons.
It was in the person of Sir James that the family was
ennobled. By charter of date 1445, he was created

Lord Hamilton, and his manor house of "The Orchard," in the barony of Cadzow was erected into his chief messuage, with the name of Hamilton which it still bears. In 1474, when at an advanced age, Lord Hamilton married the Princess Mary, eldest daughter of James II., King of Scotland, and widow of Thomas Boyd, Earl of Arran. By this connection his descendants came to be declared in Parliament, on the demise of James V., in the event of the death of Mary Queen of Scots, next heirs to the Crown, and have, in consequence, been ever since regarded as a branch of the royal family. Buchanan and some of his followers represent the Hamiltons as dependants on the Douglases, and as becoming great by betraying them to James II., who murdered the Earl of Douglas in Stirling Castle with his own hand, although he had a safeguard. It is further asserted that James III. forced the wife of Boyd, Earl of Arran, to forsake her husband, and marry Lord Hamilton. These statements, there is reason to believe, were invidious on the part of Buchanan, and made in order to please his patron the Earl of Murray, a great enemy of the Hamiltons. Boetius says, that the first daughter of James II. was married to Lord Boyd, who had by her a son and a daughter, and that after the death of Lord Boyd, this daughter of James II. was married to Lord Hamilton; in that way the Hamiltons are " decorit in the King's blood." This edition of Boetius was translated by Bellenden, who, being contemporary with the lady, is better authority than Buchanan, who lived a century after. It is to the praise of the first Lord Hamilton that in 1460, he founded a college in the University of Glasgow—the first college in Scotland founded by a layman.

The death of King James V. in 1542 left only an

infant of five days old between James, third Lord
Hamilton, second Earl of Arran, and the throne. He
was at once chosen regent of the Kingdom and tutor
to the young Queen, and declared to be "second person in the realm"—a position which carried with it
something of royal style. He signed or subscribed
his name as "James G.," or simply "James," and
wrote himself, "James, by the Grace of God, Earl of
Arran and Lord Hamilton, Governor and Prince of
Scotland." He held his high offices till 1554, when
he resigned them in favour of the Queen-mother,
Mary of Guise, receiving in return from King Henry
II. of France a grant of the Duchy of Chatelherault.
His nearness to the throne, his great following, and
large possessions, left him still a person of such mark
that his eldest son, the Earl of Arran, as he was
called, was proposed at one time as the husband of
Queen Mary of Scotland, and at another time as the
husband of Queen Elizabeth of England. The career
which opened with such high aspirations came to a
sad and untimely end ; the Earl was afflicted with
madness in 1562, and never recovered his reason,
although he lived till 1609. His father, the first
Duke of Chatelherault, dying in 1575, his second
son, Lord John Hamilton, the lay abbot or commen-
dator of Arbroath, became virtual head of the house,
and as such was, in 1599, created Marquis of Hamilton. He died in 1604, being succeeded by his son
James, the second Marquis, who, in 1619, was created
Earl of Cambridge in England, and died in 1625.
He was succeeded by his eldest son James, the third
Marquis, who led an army of 6,000 men to the support of King Gustavus Adolphus of Sweden in
1631-32 ; and a few years later acted a conspicuous
part in the great contest between Charles I. and the
Scottish Covenanters. In 1638 he was appointed his

Majesty's Commissioner to the famous General
Assembly which met at Glasgow, the proceedings of
which are well known. In 1639, when the Scots
nation were compelled to defend by arms their civil
and religious liberty, the Marquis was sent to Scotland with a well equipped fleet, and a force of 5,000
men, while the King, at the head of 25,000 foot and
3,000 horse, advanced by land. The treaty of
Berwick, concluded on the 18th July, prevented
hostilities at that time. It was on this occasion that
his mother, Ann Cunningham, appeared on horseback
on the shore near Leith, armed with pistols, and
declared that she would shoot her son should he
attempt to land and attack his countrymen. During
the 'hostilities at this time between the Royalists,
headed by the Marquis, and the Covenanters, aided
by Lords Fleming, Montgomery, Loudon, Boyd,
Lindsay, and others, the latter party seized the
Castle of Strathaven, and compelled all the gentlemen in Clydesdale, who were suspected of favouring
the Royal cause, to give security that they would not
rise in arms. "As a reward for his services," says
Douglas, "to the King, he was created Duke of
Hamilton, Marquis of Clydesdale, Earl of Arran and
Cambridge, Lord Aven and Innerdale, by patent
dated at Oxford, 12th April, 1643, to him and the
heirs male of his body ; which failing, to his brother
and the heirs male of his body ; which failing, to the
eldest heir female of the Marquis's body without
division, and the heirs male of the body of such heir
female, they bearing the name and arms of Hamilton,
which all failing, to the nearest legitimate heir what-
soever of the Marquis." In 1648, the Duke promoted
with all his power "the engagement" entered into
by the Scots Parliament to raise an army for relief of
King Charles, who was then in the hands of the

Parliamentary army. He was appointed general of
the forces, which were hastily raised, amounting to
about 10,000 foot and 4,000 cavalry. With this
army he marched into England, and, being joined
by the English Royalists they were met at Preston
by Cromwell at the head of a strong reinforcement.
A battle took place on the 17th of August, when the
Royalists were defeated and their army dispersed.
The Duke of Hamilton capitulated with General
Lambert on assurance of safety to himself and his
followers. He was afterwards taken to Windsor
Castle and confined under a strong guard. On the
21st of December, when King Charles I. was carried
through Windsor on his way to his trial in London,
that affecting interview mentioned by historians took
place between Charles and the Duke.

After the king's execution the Duke made an escape
from Windsor, under night, but entering London he was
re-taken, and brought to trial 6th February, 1649,
and sentenced to be beheaded on Friday, the 9th of
March following. In terms of the sentence, he was
decapitated in Palace Yard, Westminster, in the 43d
year of his age, and his remains were, according to
his desire, conveyed to Scotland, and deposited in the
burial place of the family at Hamilton. As the body
came by sea to Scotland, it appears to have been
landed at Borrowstouness, and taken to Kinneil
House, as it is stated in the Kirk Session books of
Hamilton that the corpse of James, first Duke of
Hamilton, was carried in a coach from Kinneil to
Hamilton, and deposited in the family vault at the
Old Church, attended by a great assemblage of
people.

His Duchess, Lady Mary Fielding, died on the
10th of May, 1638, by whom he had three sons,
Charles, James, and William, and three daughters,

Mary, Anne, and Susanna. The three sons and eldest daughter all died young. His Grace having, therefore, no male heirs, was succeeded in his titles and estates, in terms of the patent, by his brother William, Earl of Lanark. He died in 1651 of the wounds which he had received at the battle of Worcester. The duchy of Hamilton, in terms of the patent of creation, now devolved on the daughter of the first Duke, Lady Anne, whose husband, Lord William Douglas, Earl of Selkirk, was, in 1660, created Duke of Hamilton for life. He died in 1694. The Duchess Anne, who survived till 1716, had, in 1698, resigned her titles in the King's hands in favour of her eldest son, James, Earl of Arran, who was anew created Duke of Hamilton with the precedency of 1643. In 1711, he was created Duke of Brandon in England, but the House of Lords refused him a seat or vote in Parliament, on the ground that the crown was disabled ' by the Act of Union from granting a peerage of Great Britain to any person who was a peer of Scotland before the Union. The Duke was killed in a duel in Hyde Park with Lord Mohun in 1712. He was succeeded by his eldest son, James, who, dying in 1743, was succeeded by his eldest son, James, who, in 1752, married the famous beauty, Elizabeth Gunning, and died in 1758, being succeeded by his eldest son, James George, an infant of three years old. On the death of the Duke of Douglas in 1761, the male representation of the "red" or Angus Branch of the Douglases, with the titles of Marquis of Douglas, Earl of Angus, &c., devolved on the Dukes of Hamilton, as descendants of the Duchess Anne's husband, William, Earl of Selkirk, third son of the first Marquis of Douglas. Dying in 1769, in his 15th year, James George, seventh Duke of Hamilton, was succeeded by his

only brother, Douglas, who, in 1782, took his seat in
Parliament as Duke of Brandon, the House of Lords
being now satisfied, after consultation with the twelve
Judges, that the Act of Union did not prohibit the
Crown from making a peer of Scotland a peer of
Great Britain. Duke Douglas died without issue in
1799, when the titles and estates passed to his uncle,
Archibald, the second son of James, the fifth Duke.
Duke Archibald dying in 1819, was succeeded by his
eldest son, Alexander, who, in 1810, married a
daughter of Mr Beckford of Fonthill, and died in
1852; when he was succeeded by his only son,
William Alexander Anthony Archibald, eleventh
Duke of Hamilton in the peerage of Scotland. He
died in 1863, and was succeeded by William Alexander Louis Stephen Douglas Hamilton, the present
Duke, who was born in 1845.

The French monarchs always recognised the right
of the Dukes of Hamilton to the Duchy of Chatelherault. At the time of the Treaty of Utrecht, in
1713, the Earl of Abercorn preferred a claim for the
fourth part of the revenues as heir male of the first
Duke of Chatelherault, which was overruled. In
1819, when the grandfather of the present Duke
resumed the title, and again in 1823 and 1825, the
Earl of Aberdeen, as guardian of the second Marquis
of Abercorn, then a minor, through the British
Ambassador, sent a remonstrance to the French
Government, to which evasive replies were given.
Duke Alexander and his Duchess in 1826 were
received at the Court of Charles X. as Duke and
Duchess of Chatelherault. In 1853, Lord Aberdeen
revived the Abercorn pretensions by causing a representation on the subject to be made by the British
Minister. There had been no public recognition of
the title on the part of the Imperial Court; but, in

April 1864, the Emperor Napoleon III., granted a new patent in favour of the 12th Duke of Hamilton, enjoining "the maintenance and confirmation of the hereditary title of Duke of Chatelherault, created by Henry II. of France in 1548, in favour of James Hamilton, Earl of Arran;" and in April 1866, by a solemn finding of the French Law Courts, the question was finally settled, the title being declared to belong indisputably to the Duke of Hamilton.

It is somewhat remarkable (observes our well-informed local antiquary, Mr Andrew Hamilton, Quarter) that of all the numerous families of the name of Hamilton, who at one time owned lands in Lanarkshire only two who possess estates now are really Hamiltons, by male descent—viz., John G. C. Hamilton of Dalzell, who represents the Orbieston, Rosehall, and Dalzell families; and James Hamilton, who has lately established his claim before the House of Lords, and assumed the title of Lord Belhaven and Stenton, and who represents the families of Udstoun, Wishaw, and Stevenstoun. All the others are descended from heirs-female whose husbands assumed the name of Hamilton. The head of the house, the Duke of Hamilton, is a Douglas; the representative of the Broomhill, Dalserf, and Millburn branches, a Campbell; Raploch, a Macneill; Fairholm, a Stevenson; Barncluith (Lady Ruthven), a Campbell; Blantyre Farm, a Coats; Newtoun, a Gray; and Letham, in Avendale, a Napier.

Since writing the above paragraph, it has been suggested that Andrew Hamilton of Drumclog, Avendale, and Thomas Hamilton of Shawtonhill, Glassford, may be lineally descended through heirs-male, and therefore also Hamiltons; but of this we are not certain, not knowing to what branch they belong, and cannot trace their descent further back than the beginning of the 17th century, although, to all appearance, there has been a regular succession of heirs-male in both families from. that period to the present time.

Other two families—viz., those of Silvertonhill, and Avendale and Gilkerscleugh, who once owned extensive possessions in Clydesdale are, we believe, represented at the present time by heirs male lineally descended ; but the former, Sir Robert North Collie Hamilton, enjoys only the title of Silvertonhill, without any lands ; and the latter, George John Hamilton, Major, 26th Foot, has now no lands whatever in the county, his grandfather, Daniel Hamilton of Gilkerscleugh, Sheriff-Depute of Lanarkshire, having sold Gilkerscleugh about fifty years ago to Sir Edward Colebrooke.

HAMILTON PALACE.

The Palace of Hamilton was originally a square tower about 20 feet long and 16 feet wide. The old part of the house as it now stands was erected about 1591, and about 1717 it was almost entirely rebuilt. The front, facing the south, was ornamented with pillars of the Corinthian order, and two deep wings were added, in the form of a Roman H, much in the style of Greenwich Hospital. In 1822 additions on an extensive scale were carried to completion by Alexander, tenth Duke (the present Duke's grandfather), with Mr Hamilton, as architect, and Mr Connell (builder of Burns' Monument at Ayr) as builder, which have rendered the Palace of Hamilton one of the largest and most magnificent structures of the kind in Britain. The modern part consists of a new front facing the north, 264 feet 8 inches in length, and three stories high, with an additional wing to the west, 100 feet in length, for servants' apartments. A new corridor is carried along the back of the old building, containing baths, &c. The front is adorned by a noble portico, consisting of a double row of Corinthian columns, each of one solid stone surmounted by a lofty pediment. The shaft of each column is upwards of 25 feet in height and about 3 feet 3 inches in diameter. These were each brought in the block from a quarry in Dalserf, about eight miles distant, on an immense waggon constructed for the purpose and drawn by thirty horses. The Palace stands close upon the town, on the upper border of the great valley, about half-a-mile west of the conflux of the Clyde and Avon. It is recorded as a curious statistical fact that there were employed in building the addition to the Palace, 28,056 tons $8\frac{3}{4}$ cwt. of stones, drawn by 22,528 horses. Of lime, sand, stones, wood, &c., 5,534 tons, 6 cwt., 1 qr., $7\frac{1}{2}$ lbs., drawn by 5,196 horses. In drawing 22,350 slates, 62,200 bricks, with engine ashes and coal-culm to keep down the damp, 731 horses were employed. Total days during which horses were employed for other purposes, $658\frac{1}{2}$. In the stables there are 7,976 tons of stones, drawn by 5,153 horses. Of lime, sand, slates, &c., 1,361 tons, drawn by 1,024 horses; besides 284 days of horses employed for other purposes. The stables, according to plan, are not yet completed.

INTERIOR EQUIPMENTS.

The interior equipments of the Palace are not less tasteful or magnificent than its exterior, and are a fair counterpart of the gorgeous pile in which they are contained. Amongst the works of art, "Daniel

in the Lion's Den" is a noble picture—the subject of
Wordsworth's sonnet—

" Amid a fertile region, green with wood
And fresh with rivers, well doth it become
The ducal owner, in his palace home
To naturalise this tawny lion brood ;
Children of art, that claim strange brotherhood,
Couched in their den, with those that roam at large
Over the burning wilderness, and charge
The wind with terror while they roar for food.
Satiate were these ; and still—to eye and ear ;
Hence, while we gage a more enduring fear !
Yet is the prophet calm, nor would the cave
Daunt him—if his companion now bedroused,
Outstretched and listless, were by hunger roused ;
Man placed him here, and God, he knows, can save."

The portrait of Charles I. in armour on a white
horse, and of the Earl of Denbigh in a shooting dress
standing by a tree, with the muzzle of a gun grasped
in his right hand, and the butt of it resting on the
ground, with a little black boy on the opposite side
of the tree pointing out the game—both by Vandyke
—are also masterpieces of art. Without going into
detail, there may be mentioned an Entombment of
Christ, by Poussin ; an Ascension piece, by Georgi-
one ; a dying Madonna, by Corregio ; the Circumcision,
signed Lucas Cortonensis ; the Misers, Quinten
Matsys ; Assumption of our Lady, Sandro Bottocelli ;
painted for the Church of San Pietro, Florence, on the
commission of Matteo Palmieri, who gave the whole
scheme of the work. The Assumption contains a representation of the zones of heaven, the patriarchs, pro-
phets, apostles, evangelists, martyrs, confessors, doctors,
virgins, and hierarchies. Matteo and his wife are
represented on their knees in the foreground ; in the
distance is a view of the city of Florence. Vasari
says envious detractors of the painter charged him
and his patron with heresy, and the work was inter-

dicted and covered from view. A laughing Boy, by
L. Da Vinci ; and an admirable portrait of Napoleon
by David, painted from life, by permission granted
to the Duke of Hamilton—are well-known works
of art of great value. The west stair-case contains a
large altar-piece by Girolami dai Libri from San
Lionardo nel Monte, near Verona, of the Castieri
family, with a Madonna and a child, placed in a chair
above them. In the breakfast room is a picture by
Giacomo da Puntormo of Joseph in Egypt receiving
his father and his brothers ; into which is introduced
the portrait of Beronzino. In the same room is a
portrait by Antonelli of Mycena in 1474. This is still
in a state of admirable preservation. The great
gallery and principal apartments contain also a large
collection of family portraits and other paintings by
Vandyke, Kneller, Rubens, Corregio, Guido,
Rembrandt, Titian, Poussin, Spagnoletti, Reynolds,
Hamilton, &c. Here, if anywhere, is

" An art akin to nature's self,
So mighty in its means, we stand prepared
To see the life as lively mocked, as ever
Still sleep mocked death."

A number of antique vases adorn the principal
rooms, particularly one in the new dining room, of
Giallo-Antico, in the form of a tripod, of great
beauty, and of extraordinary dimensions, being 5 ft.
3 in. in height, 14 ft. 3 in. in circumference, and $9\frac{1}{2}$
in. deep. The vase itself is supported by a circular
central pillar of beautiful form, richly carved and
fluted, and with three square fluted pilasters at the
sides, each resting on a lion's foot, and terminating
with a lion's head—the whole standing on a vase of
beautiful African marble. In the breakfast room and
small drawing room are two slabs of porphyry upon

gilt bronze legs—formerly comprising part of an
altar-piece at Rome. Both slabs are of oriental
porphyry, of equal size, and of great beauty. In an
adjoining room there is a cabinet covered with a slab
of malachite of most splendent lustre. There are
also a great many antique cabinets in the different
apartments, enriched with Mosaic and all sorts of
precious stones ; particularly, a casket of ebony ornamented with gilt bronze, and oriental stones in relief,
formerly belonging to the Medici family. At the
upper end of the gallery is Duke Alexander's ambas-
sadorial throne, brought from his embassy at St.
Petersburgh ; and on the walls on each side of the
throne are two capital portraits of George III. and
Queen Charlotte, painted soon after their marriage.
Fronting the throne, at the other end of the gallery,
is a magnificent large architectural door of black
marble, the pediment being supported by two
oriental columns of green porphyry, unique in their
kind, and supposed to be the finest of that material
in Europe. The two oriental black porphyry
columns were purchased by Alexander, tenth Duke
of Hamilton, at Rome, from an individual who had
them as a favour in gift from Braschi Pius VII.
They were taken by his Holiness's orders from the
Church of St. Georgio in Viterbo, which church was
built out of the ruins of the Basilica di Semproneo.
These columns originally formed an ornament to
that ancient Basilica, one of the most celebrated of
Ancient Rome. The collection of pictures numbers
not less than 1000 pieces, of which 100 are at
Chatelherault. The value of the prints alone, none
of which are exhibited to strangers, has been estimated at from £10,000 to £15,000. Some of them
have never been unfolded. Many of the cabinets are
worth £1,500 ; and a single table has been estimated

at £4,000. The value of the plate is over £50,000. In the drawing room are two marble columns from Astracan, said by geologists to be unique, and which are valued at £40,000. The present Duke, when recently in Venice, acquired two magnificent bottle-shaped vases, composed of tortoise shell inlaid with ivory, and studded with turquoise and other precious stones. The vases are four feet in height. They are placed on pedestals two feet in height, supported by three negroes in a kneeling posture. His Grace, at the same time, procured two figures of negresses, five feet in height, beautifully painted in full Eastern costume; mounted on pedestals two feet high, and which are placed on the Eastern staircase.

GREAT HALL.

The principal apartments besides the entrance hall, are—the tribune, a spacious saloon with lofty and highly ornamented lantern roof, from which many of the principal rooms enter; a dining room, 71 feet by 30; a library and drawing room. Next the drawing room is the Great Hall, entered from the steps under the portico of the north front; it is 54 feet square and 42 feet high from the floor to the roof; the walls, from floor to ceiling, being of polished sand-stone. Over the two fire-places are the ducal arms, carved in stone. The upper portion is enriched with carved cross beams and cornice, supported by sixteen fluted pilasters with capitals all of polished sand-stone. The floor is paved with Sienna and black marble. There are here five colossal bronze statues of L'Apollon du Belveder, La Diane, Le Gladiateur, L'Hercule Commode, L'Antinous Belveder, each on a black marble pedestal three feet high. These statues were cast in Italy early in the sixteenth century by order of Francois I. in moulds taken from the original statues in Rome. They were afterwards acquired by Nicolas Merville, Secretary of State. At the Revolution they were removed to Paris, and purchased there by Alexander, Duke of Hamilton, and placed in the palace. There is also here a colossal bronze bust of Alexander, Duke of Hamilton, by Thomas Campbell; besides other busts, vases of porphyry, rare marbles, &c.

GRAND STAIR-CASE.

The steps, balusters, and rails are all of pure black marble from Galway in Ireland. The stairs branch right and left from the first landing, terminating at a landing leading from the Great Hall to the tapestry rooms. This is also of black marble. Each rail is formed of one piece, and the first landing is a solid slab, measuring ten feet by seven feet. The long landing or passage is supported from below by two colossal figures in bronze by Soyer of Paris. The floor is paved with Sienna and black marble, and the walls are of polished sand-stone, similar to the Great Hall, carried to the roof. The ceiling is arched and richly ornamented with plaster work, the family arms, &c. On the side walls are hanging full length portraits of the Emperor Napoleon III. and the Empress Eugenie by Winterhalter. There are also here three antique busts—Vespasian in basalt and oriental alabaster; the Emperor Augustus, in Egyptian porphyry and gilt metal ornaments; Tiberias, in Egyptian porphyry with gilt metal ornaments. These busts are on ebonised pedestals, ornamented with pietra dura and gilt metal work.

TAPESTRY ROOMS.

The walls of these rooms are hung with very fine Italian tapestry, the subject of which is taken from Tasso's "Jerusalem Delivered." The ceiling is in compartments richly gilt and coloured. The doors, windows, &c., are white and gold, the chairs and sofas richly gilt and covered in tapestry, the cabinets, tables, vases, &c., are of the choicest kind, corresponding with the other portions of the Palace. We may mention a Damascene table of Milanese work of the sixteenth century, purchased at Prince Soltykoff's sale at Paris for 800 guineas. It would be beyond our sphere to attempt to enumerate all the precious and costly articles of furniture in this princely Palace.

GALLERY AND OLD STATE ROOMS.

The gallery is 120 feet by 20, and 20 feet high. The ceiling is in compartments, with portions of the family arms, richly gilt and coloured. The walls are covered with dark oak panels. Leaving the gallery, entrance is obtained to the old state rooms, the walls of which are panelled to correspond with those of the gallery. These magnificent chambers contain a superb variety of costly cabinets, in Mosaic work, Japan Lac, Buhl, &c. ; besides a collection of sumptuous furniture and pictures.

THE BECKFORD LIBRARY.

Adjoining the old staterooms is the Beckford library. The room was specially arranged for this celebrated collection, after the decease, in 1844, of Wm. Beckford. Esq., of Fonthill (the author of "Vathek") whose daughter married Alexander, tenth Duke of Hamilton, and by whom it was formed. The collection consists of over 15,000 volumes, amongst which are many rare editions of the early authors—all in the finest condition. The room is T shaped. The ceiling is arched, pierced for lights from the roof. All round the room over the cases (which are entirely of cedar wood) is a rich scagliola cornice, supported by polished Peterhead granite pilasters on a scagliola base. Over the centre of the T is a circular dome with a light in roof, around which are painted allegorical figures representing literature, music, painting, and architecture. There are here four full-length portraits of the Beckford family— Miss Beckford (afterwards Duchess of Hamilton), by Phillips; William Beckford, Esq., by Romney; his father, Alderman Beckford, by Sir Joshua Reynolds ; and Peter Beckford, their ancestor, Governor of Jamaica in 1692. These pictures are fixed in panels to the wall over the fire-places, supported below on rich marble slabs ; above is a cornice of scagliola, supported from the marble slab at the back by pilasters of Aberdeen granite ; in front by columns of antique Egyptian granite, with gilt metal capitals. Besides this library there is the family collection of books—altogether upwards of 25,000 volumes, and 800 volumes of MSS. In the wing leading from the other end of the gallery are the

DUCHESS' PRIVATE APARTMENTS.

These are most tastefully decorated in white and gold, and are richly furnished. Included amongst the valuable furniture is a secretaire, a bureau, and a work table, formerly belonging to Maria Antoinette of France, and said to be the finest specimens of inlaid-work extant. They were manufactured by Reisner of Paris, the metal work by Goutière. The catalogue of the South Kensington Loan Exhibition says—" In the three specialities is displayed the utmost perfection of French decorative art ; and, in all probability, the suite of furniture as a whole is the most important and beautiful work of its kind produced in the age of Louis XVI."

THE CHARTER ROOM.

The charter room contains, besides the family charters, a number of valuable manuscript letters, including the correspondence of Charles the First, the Duke of Lauderdale, and others, with the first Duke of Hamilton and his brother, the Earl of Lanark. Many other curious relics are deposited here, as, for instance, the ring given by Queen Mary previous to her execution, to Lord John Hamilton, afterwards Marquis of Hamilton, and the veritable gun with which Hamilton of Bothwell Haugh fired the shot which proved fatal to the Regent Murray at Linlithgow.

MISCELLANEOUS.

The Palace and main avenues are lighted with gas. The Duke Alexander, amongst other improvements, at considerable expense provided a copious supply of pure water for the use of the Palace. A large tank and filter were constructed on the heights at Chatelherault. The water is conveyed by pipes into cisterns on the roof of the Palace. Pipes are also laid round the exterior of the building as a provision in case of fire. Recently the town's gravitation water has also been added, so that should unfortunately a fire ever take place, it is expected the provision will be equal to the emergency.

The stables stand between the Palace and town, and are in every way worthy of the splendid edifice of which they are an appropriate accompaniment.

The gardens belong to a recent date. During the season of 1861, a new geometrical flower plot was formed at the eastern wing of the Palace. It covers nearly an acre of ground, and is surrounded by a massive balustrade wall, with a handsome fountain in the centre. The new kitchen and forcing garden was formed about the same time. The garden is about 5½ acres in extent, and contains a range of hot houses 370 feet in length and 14 in breadth. Situated on a gently sloping bank, as seen from Cadzow Bridge the stretch of greenhouses, &c., present an imposing appearance.

QUEEN MARY AT THE PALACE.

The associations of the Palace are many of them necessarily interesting. A touching episode is furnished in the narrative of the visit of the unfortunate Queen of Scots after her escape from Loch Leven and at the time of the Langside disaster. The Queen, after her delivery from the keep of Kinross, rode to the Castle of Niddry, near Linlithgow, and next day, the number of her followers increasing, she went on to Hamilton Palace. According to Hill Burton, among the chiefs who had here assembled, besides Seton and the Hamiltons, were Herries, Sommerville, Argyle, Cassilis, Fleming, Ross, Eglinton, and Rothes. They had soon around them six hundred men in fighting array. Hamilton Palace had the aspect of a Court well guarded by troops. The opportunity was taken to revoke the Queen's abdication, with all the business that had followed upon it. The Queen's followers naturally looked around for some stronger position than Hamilton, and an attempt to gain Dunbar Castle having failed, Dumbarton, held by Lord Fleming, was the next recourse. It involved a march close by Glasgow, where the Regent Murray was stationed; but, as the Queen's force was the larger of the two, it was resolved to take this risk. After the battle, the decisive character of which sealed the fate of Scotland, the Queen rode off towards the Border, and in a short time was a prisoner in the hands of Elizabeth. Albeit, her son, James VI., is said to have frequently enjoyed the sports of the field at Cadzow, and the Hamiltons

in subsequent reigns were prominent figures. Until
recent years, there is no further notable event connected with royalty and the Palace to record—

> Old times were changed, old manners gone,
> A stranger fill'd the Stuarts' throne.

OTHER ROYAL VISITORS.

Of distinguished visitors at the Palace in recent
years, may be mentioned the Duchess of Kent (the
mother of Her Most Gracious Majesty), in 1851; the
late Queen of Holland, 1857; the Empress Eugenie,
in 1860; the Duc de Bordeaux (Henry V.); and the
Emperor Napoleon.

VISIT OF THE PRINCE OF WALES.

On 13th January of this year (1878), H.R.H. the
Prince of Wales arrived at the Palace on a
visit to the Duke and Duchess of Hamilton. The
Princes Imperial of Austria and France, with other distinguished personages, were invited to meet H.R.H.,
and for a week the Palace was once more the centre of
gaiety and festivity. The early meeting of Parliament
curtailed the royal visit to one of four days, but the
most was made of the brief space, and before his
departure the Heir Apparent had seen enough of the
district to charm him with its scenery—its fine timber
especially exciting surprise and admiration—and
of the inhabitants to gratify him with the
sincere heartiness and cordiality of their loyalty.
The Prince's well-known agricultural proclivities led
him to Merryton, where Mr Drew showed his famous
Clydesdales, passing under royal review, "Prince
of Wales," "Lord Harry," and over one hundred
mares, colts, and fillies, and providing a sight which,
in the words of H.R.H., could nowhere else be seen

in the world. The Prince Imperial of France got on
the back of "Lord Harry," which had never been
ridden before ; and the bystanders looked on as he
scampered round the yard, hardly knowing whether
to admire or reprove the wildness of the feat. On
Monday, the royal party shot over the home policies,
and on Tuesday found their way to the High Parks.
In marked contrast to the previous day, rain, accompanied by a high wind, fell all the morning, and continued during the remainder of the day. Undeterred,
the Prince of Wales, the Crown Prince of Austria,
the Prince Imperial, Prince Esterhazy, Count
Jaraczewski, Count Bombelle, the Duc de Bassano,
and three other gentlemen, left the Palace at eleven
o'clock. Mr Tait, the head keeper, and assistants had
gone on to Larkhall an hour before. Along the route
to the shooting ground the royal cavalcade attracted
much attention, and were cheered at different
points where crowds had assembled. Entering
the grounds at Larkhall, the party shot through the
Captain's Wood on to Belvedere, which they also
exhausted. So plentiful were the game, the services of
the beaters were hardly needed, and the difficulty was
to shoot the animals that came within range. At
Chatelherault a halt was called for lunch. The storm
was at its height, and the party remained at the
chateau for some time. A start was eventually
made, the party having to drive for some distance.
After crossing the river at the ornamental
bridge, the peeps of scenery from both sides of which
were greatly admired, they lingered for a time
amid the hoary ruins of the Castle of Cadzow,
which here crown the precipitous banks of the stream,
and then they passed on to the Oaks and the White
Cattle in the chase beyond. It would be difficult to
describe the surprise of the sportsmen in unexpectedly

finding themselves surrounded by so many grand specimens of the monarch of the forest. In the White Cattle, too, they evinced the greatest interest. They concluded the day's shooting in Ramsay's cover. The roe deer which were met with were very wild, some of them leaping over the keepers' heads. The Prince of Wales brought down one of the deer, the Prince Imperial of France another, and three fell to other guns. The Duke of Hamilton was present, but confined himself to attending to the wants of his guests. The bag for four hours' work and ten guns was the largest ever made in a similar space of time within the memory of the oldest keeper. In the evening, the Duke and Duchess gave a ball in the Tribune of the Palace, which was attended by the royal party and several hundred guests. Such a galaxy of beauty and fashion had not assembled in the same noble chamber for years before; and

"When to the trembling string
The dance gaed thro' the lighted ha."

with the bright dresses of the ladies and the blaze of uniforms the scene was brilliant and dazzling. On Wednesday the party for a short time were out on the Logans, and at night took their departure.

The inhabitants—the private character of the visit, and the brief intimation of the hour of departure leaving little time for preparation—yet succeeded in making a most creditable display of loyalty. The public buildings were illuminated, and private houses lighted up. In honour of their noble Colonel, the Queen's Own Yeomanry furnished a guard of honour, and at the Central Railway Station the 16th Lanark Rifles, under Colonel Austine, were drawn up. Inside the platform was a most respectable crowd of three thousand people. Opposite the saloon carriage in

4

which His Royal Highness was to travel were posted the Provost, Magistrates, and Town Council, it having been previously ascertained that the Prince would be pleased to receive an address from the Corporation. The address, which was presented in graceful terms by Provost Forrest to His Royal Highness, ran :—

"We, the Provost, Magistrates, and Town Council of the burgh of Hamilton desire to avail ourselves of this opportunity of renewing the assurances of our attachment and loyalty to your august mother and to your Royal Higness, and the other members of your illustrious family, under whose enlightened and paternal government the people of these realms have enjoyed so much prosperity and happiness.

"We learned with much pleasure that your Royal Highness was to visit the Duke and Duchess of Hamilton, and our regret is that circumstances have prevented you from prolonging your stay ; but it is our hope that you will at no distant date renew your acquaintance with a district fraught with many interesting associations, and characterised by devoted loyalty to the throne.

"We desire to express the hope that your Royal Highness and your illustrious and most estimable wife, and your Royal children, will long continue to occupy your elevated social positions, and, endowed with health and other blessings, that you will be enabled to discharge the duties which these positions entail.

"Signed, in name and by appointment of the Magistrates and Town Council of Hamilton, this 16th day of January, 1878,

"J. C. FORREST, Provost."

His Royal Highness expressed the pleasure it afforded him to receive the address, to which he stated a reply would be forwarded in the usual way. He then entered the carriage amidst loud cheers, which he repeatedly acknowledged, and was followed by the Prince Imperial of France. The train was then backed out of the station, and having been shunted on to the centre line of rails, it slowly steamed past the platform, the public on both sides having the while a good view of the occupants of the train. The Prince of Wales and Prince Imperial held their hats in their hands until the train was clear of the station, and acknowledged the hearty cheers with which they were greeted. The band played the National Anthem, and the cheering was renewed again and again. Provost Forrest afterwards received the following reply to the address :—

"Sandringham, King's Lynn,
19th January, 1878.

"Sir,—I am desired by the Prince of Wales to thank you, and through you the Magistrates and Town Council of the Burgh of Hamilton, for the expressions of loyalty towards the Queen, himself, and the Royal Family contained in your address to His Royal Highness of the 16th inst.

"The Prince further commands me to thank you for the reception you gave him at Hamilton, and to say how he regrets that important duties in England prevented his making a longer stay in your loyal burgh.

"His Royal Highness hopes, however, at some future period to renew his acquaintance with a district which, as you rightly say, is fraught with many interesting associations.

"I have the honour to be, Sir, your most obedient servant,

"D. M. PROBYN, Major-General,
Comptroller and Treasurer of the Household of
His Royal Highness the Prince of Wales.

"To J. C. Forrest, Esq., Provost of Hamilton,"

The annexed table shows the total results of the royal and ducal sport :—

	Poli-cies.	High Parks.	Log-ans.	Draf-fan.	Home Farm.	Quar ter.	Dech-mont.	Total.
Pheasants, ...	83	171	59	25	101	96	110	615
Partridges, ...	..	1	2	19	20	4	20	66
Hares, ...	19	64	87	500	228	121	223	1249
Rabbits,........	626	1002	641	520	121	345	121	3376
Woodcocks,....	2	14	6	3	1	3	1	30
Deer, ...	..	5	3	..	..	1	..	33
Sundries, ...	1	7	3	9	6	1	6	33
Total,........	731	1264	801	1076	477	571	486	5402
Guns,........	9	13	11	10	12	7	5	66

This had never been equalled in any previous season. The following took part in the shooting : — H.R.H. The Prince of Wales, H.I.H.

Crown Prince of Austria, H.I.H. Prince Imperial of France, Prince Louis Esterhazy, Duke of Hamilton, Duke of Manchester, Duke de Bassano, Lord Rendlesham, Lord Mandeville, Count Jaraczewski, Count Bombelle, Mr Montague Guest, Mr Vaughan, Mr Cooper, Colonel Campbell, Major Coghill, The Hon. Hanbury Lennox, Colonel Teesdale.

THE MAUSOLEUM.

The Mausoleum, another of Duke Alexander's creations, is situated on a beautifully formed terrace, raised to the north-west of the Palace, from which it is distant about a quarter of a mile. It is to a considerable extent enclosed by rows of stately beeches, varied at intervals by luxuriant shrubbery, but from its great altitude, being nearly 120 feet high, it towers far above the objects by which it is surrounded. The base covers an area of somewhere about 110 feet diameter. The structure is a composition of Roman architecture, most of the details being developed in the purest style. The mausoleum may be said to consist of three several storeys or compartments placed upon a surbase formed by colossal steps rising several feet, above which is a massive stylobate or basement, in the western portion of which is the entrance to the chapel. From this stylobate rises a dado, whose sides are panelled and pilastered. This is perhaps the most pretentious of the three storeys and exhibits great skill and elaborate finish. The panels are formed by single slabs, of gigantic proportions, and the effect produced is strikingly imposing. The super-structure is a huge plinth of plain polished stone, with the guilloche or fretband boldly indented and channelled. The whole is surmounted by a dome which rises eighteen feet above the plinth. The vaulted basement constitutes what may be termed

the ground storey of this splendid temple of the
dead.

In deference, it is understood, to popular ideas, the
entrance to the catacombs is placed in the east. This
portion forms the front of the mausoleum, and is
built in a piazza-like form. It consists of three
massive arches executed in rustic work, the frontage
stretching some 80 or 90 feet. On the keystones are
exquisitely carved masks, the work of Mr Handyside
Ritchie of Edinburgh, representing Life, Death, and
Immortality. Life is adorned with a chaplet of fruit
and flowers ; and on the lower portion of the stone is
part of a clock-dial, with the indicator pointing to the
hour of twelve. Death is crowned with poppy heads
and a variety of flowers ; over the mouth is placed
the dread seal of everlasting silence, a finger rising
obliquely upwards over the lips ; the eyes are for
ever closed in "the sleep that knows no waking,"
and the expression of the face is awe-striking and
effective. Immortality forms a vivid contrast to the
other masks, especially that of Death ; the head is
crowned with lilies, and the brow encircled with the
serpent, emblematic of eternity ; while immediately
above is the Greek symbol of immortality, a butterfly.

Passing through the centre archway we are speedily
in the vaults or catacombs. Mr David Hamilton
planned this portion of the basement ; and the grov-
ing and vaulting are certainly splendid models of
masonry. A solid pillar of stone in the centre receives
the springing of all the arches, thus supporting the
fan-groining. By the dim light emitted through the
door-way, the visitor is made aware that many of the
recesses are occupied by the remains of Scotland's
premier Dukes. Early in 1852, the bodies which had
previously rested for centuries in the old Church of
Hamilton—once situated in the immediate vicinity of

the Palace, but now levelled to the dust, and every
trace of its existence removed—were transferred to
the vaults of the new Mausoleum, where they now
repose. There are thirteen of these, and there have
since been interred the body of the late Duke in 1863
and that of his mother some few years before.

Leaving the vaults, we find the piazza terminated
on each side by handsome stairs, which lead to the
chapel of the Mausoleum. At the top of these stairs
are two colossal lions, beautifully cut in freestone by
Mr A. H. Ritchie, which surmount the piazza, and
are placed so as to command the arches that lead to
the catacombs beneath. To these majestic guardians
of the dead, the spirit of sentinelship has been
imparted by the artist in a most masterly style. The
entrance to the chapel is from the western side. In
approaching, the eye is attracted by an inscription, in
bold raised characters, and by the elegance of the door
of the chapel. The inscription is as follows :—

HOC MONVMENTVM
SIBI ET SVIS
EXTRENDVM CVRAVIT
ALEXANDER
DVX HAMILTONII DECIMVS

"Alexander, tenth Duke of Hamilton caused this
monument to be erected for him and his." The chapel
door is in bronze, is a superb work of art, and reflects
much credit on Sir John Steell, R.S.A., by whom it
was executed. It comprises *fac-similes* of various
panels forming the celebrated gates of Ghiberti, in the
Baptistry of Florence. Critics who have seen both
original and copy, bear testimony not only to the
beauty, but the correctness of the counterfeit present-
ments. There are six panels, each of which illustrate,
in mixed alto and basso-relievo, interesting Scripture
subjects : the Queen of Sheba's reception by Solomon ;

David Slaying Goliath, and Flight of the Philistines ; Isaac blessing Jacob, and Esau entering from the Hunt ; Joseph and his brethren in Egypt, and the finding of the Cup in Benjamin's sack ; Moses on the mount, and the carrying of the Ark across the Jordan. The castings are the first of the kind executed in Scotland, and are not the least creditable of the great sculptor's work.

Inside the chapel the *tout ensemble* is exceedingly imposing and solemn. The chapel is circular, the walls being effectively broken up by numerous niches, wreaths, and other appropriate decorations. A "dim religious light" is admitted from the dome by means of an immense sheet of plate glass, from 12 to 15 feet in diameter. The subdued rays streaming in through this opening fall with an awe-inspiring influence which is deepened by the immense altitude of the chapel, while the powerful echo from the dome responds to the slightest whisper or the gentlest footfall. A splendid effect is produced by the ornate character of the floor. It is laid in mosaic, arranged in a geometrical design, and is composed of jasper, white and yellow marbles, with radiations of red and green porphyry, and divisional bands of black marble. The whole is picturesque and artistic, both in colour and arrangement. In the first storey, so to speak, there are four principal recesses with pilasters surmounted by a plain frieze. In the largest recess, and exactly opposite the entrance to the chapel, is placed the sarcophagus which contains the embalmed body of the tenth Duke. It rests upon a plain but massive pedestal of black marble. The sarcophagus consists of two ponderous pieces of basalt, and is one of those precious Memphian relics of antiquity which have from time to time been recovered from the land of the Pharaohs. It was originally intended for the

British Museum, but owing to a dispute about the price, it fell into the hands of the Duke Alexander. On the upper portion or lid, a female face of colossal features, but noble expression, looks upward, while the surface from head to foot, is covered with various figures and hieroglyphics. The sarcophagus and portion of the marble upon which the sarcophagus rests bears the following inscription :—

ALEXANDER,
HAMILTONII, BRANDONII, ET CASTELLEROTII,
DUX,
NAT. D. III. OCT., A. MDCCLXVII.
OBIT. D. XVIII. AUGUST, A. MDCCCLII.

Above the recess in which the sarcophagus is placed, the Hamilton arms are sculptured. Immediately above the pilasters previously alluded to, there are a series of oval shields, with mottoes, surmounted by exquisitely carved cherub heads, also the work of Mr A. H. Ritchie. The stone used was selected from quarries near Glasgow, the lower portion having been built with blocks from the Duke's own quarries.

The architect was Mr David Bryce, R.S.A., and the cost over £100,000.

CHATELHERAULT.

The chateau or summer palace of Chatelherault is finely situated on a commanding eminence on the banks of Avon, opposite the ruins of Cadzow Castle. It fitly terminates the fine avenue of trees which stretches in direct vista from here to the Palace, and thence on to Bothwell. The chateau, with its turrets and extended front, looks more spacious than it really is. The principal gamekeeper occupies one wing and the other is reserved for the use of the Duke when out shooting in the neighbourhood. The kennels are also located here. The walls of the chief apartments exhibit exquisite specimens of French decorative art, of the era of Louis Quatorze, in wood-carving and stucco. The truth-to-nature, lightness, delicacy, and elegance of these plaster pictures are exceedingly pleasing and impressive. They consist of scenes of rural life, of fruits and flowers, of mythologic figures, and others

> Smacking of Flora and the country green,
> Dance and provencal song, and sunburnt mirth.

THE OAKS AND ABORIGINAL BREED OF CATTLE.

The venerable oaks of Cadzow—the remains of the great Caledonian forest, which in olden times extended over the whole of upper Clydesdale and the valley of the Tweed as far as the English Border—are well-known to all lovers of leafy solitudes, for their boundless contiguity of shade. But besides the ancient ruin of Cadzow Castle, which overhangs the steep banks of the Avon, this umbrageous forest affords shelter to other relics of the past, in the shape of the last surviving descendants of the wild cattle that formerly roamed through the forest solitudes of Northern Britain. Their claim to be the last of the race is perhaps shared with the white cattle at Chillingham, in Northumberland, but owing to the erratic fancy of a park-keeper about the beginning of the present century, the specific distinction of black muzzles and ears, which are the beauty of the Cadzow cattle, was weeded out from the Chillingham herd— preference being given to an accidental pink-eared strain. Formerly herds of these white wild cattle existed at Gisburne, at Wollaton, at Chartley, and in the chase of Drumlanrig—all of them possessing the distinguishing characteristic of black ears and muzzle. But these have gradually disappeared. Sir Walter

Scott, when passing a summer in the Upper Ward,
availed himself of Cadzow to introduce these denizens
of the forest into his spirited ballad of "Cadyow
Castle"—

> "Mightiest of all the beasts of chase
> That roam in woody Caledon,
> Crashing the forest in his race,
> The mountain bull comes thundering on."

These verses Thomas Campbell speaks of as
"perpetually ringing in his imagination." But
although the white cattle of Cadzow retain at the
present day many of the instincts and habits of their
wilder progenitors, they have assuredly become much
more discreetly behaved than in Scott's days. The
"mountain bull" seldom, except at certain seasons of
the year, displays much disposition to attack strangers,
and when, according to annual custom, some of the
herd are shot down in the winter, the slaughter is a
very matter of fact performance. It is quite in the
fitness of things that, as relics of antiquity, these
white steers should be slain among venerable oaks at
Christmas-tide. The oak was the sacred tree of
Druidical worship, and at the festival of the winter
solstice in honour of the Sun-god, the ancient Britons,
accompanied by their priests, sallied forth to gather
the mistletoe from its branches. "When the oak
was reached on which the mistletoe grew, two white
bulls were bound to the tree, and the chief Druid,
clothed in white, ascended, and, with a golden knife,
cut the sacred plant. The bulls, and often also
human victims, were then sacrificed." The oaks
cover several hundred acres. Many of the trees
have attained to an enormous size, measuring 36
feet in circumference; others are gnarled and in the last
stages of decay. Permission to visit the oaks and white
cattle is by order, which can be had on application to
the Duke's officials. Pic-nic parties occasionally

frequent the grove, and to all such the famous "boss tree," which is capable of containing at one time eight individuals, is an object of interest and attraction.

In Sir William Jardine's "Naturalist's Library" there is a very interesting account of the Hamilton breed of white cattle, for which the learned baronet acknowledges to have been indebted to Robert Brown, Esq., Chamberlain to His Grace the Duke of Hamilton, and which we extract :—

"This very ancient and peculiar breed of cattle has been long kept up with great care by the noble family of Hamilton, in a chase in the vicinity of their splendid seat at Hamilton, in the Middle Ward of the County of Lanark. They are generally believed to be the remains of the ancient breed of white cattle which were found on the island when the Romans first visited it, and which they represent as then running wild in the woods. The chase in which they browse was formerly a park or forest attached to the Royal Castle of Cadzow, where the ancient British kings of Strathclyde, and subsequently kings of Scotland, used frequently to reside and to hold their courts. The oaks with which the park is studded over, are evidently very ancient, and many of them are of enormous size. Some of these are English oaks, and are supposed to have been planted by King David, first Earl of Huntingdon, about the year 1140. The chase is altogether of princely dimensions and appearance, amounting to upwards of 1300 Scotch acres. The number of white cattle at present kept is upwards of sixty. Great care is taken to prevent the domestic bull from crossing the breed ; and if accidentally a cross should take place, the young is destroyed. In their general habits they resemble the fallow-deer more than any other domestic animal. Having been exposed, without shade or covering

of any sort, to the rigours of our climate from
time immemorial, they are exceedingly hardy ; and
having never been caught or subjected to the
sway of man, they are necessarily peculiarly wild
and untractable.   Their affection for their young,
like that of many other animals in a wild or half-
wild state, is excessive.   When dropt they care-
fully conceal them among long grass or weeds in some
brushwood or thicket, and approach them cautiously
twice or thrice a day, for the purpose of supplying
them with the necessary nourishment.   On these
occasions it is not a little dangerous to approach the
place of retreat, the parent cow being seldom at any
great distance, and always attacking any person or
animal approaching it with the utmost resolution and
fury.   The calves, when unexpectedly approached,
betray great trepidation, by throwing their ears
back close upon their necks, and lying squat down
upon the ground.   When hard pressed they have been
known to run at their keepers in a butting menacing
attitude in order to force their retreat.   The young
are produced at all seasons of the year, but chiefly in
spring.   The mode of catching the calves is to steal
upon them whilst slumbering or sleeping in their retreat when they are a day or two old, and put a cloth
over their mouths to prevent them crying, and then
carry them off to a place of safety, without the reach of
the herd, otherwise the cry of the calf would attract the
dam, and she by loud bellowing would bring the whole
flock to the spot, to attack the keeper in the most
furious manner.   These cattle are seldom seen scat-
tering themselves indiscriminately over the pasture
like other breeds of cattle, but are generally observed
to feed in a flock.   They are very chary of being
approached by strangers, and seem to have the power
of smelling them at a great distance.   When any one

approaches them unexpectedly, they generally scamper off to a little distance to the leeward, and then turn round in a body to smell him. In these gambols they invariably affect circles, and when they do make an attack—which is seldom the case—should they miss the object of their aim, they never return upon it, but run straight forward without ever venturing to look back. The only method of slaughtering these animals is by shooting at them. When the keepers approach them for this purpose they seem perfectly aware of their danger, and always gallop away with great speed in a dense mass, preserving a profound silence, and generally keeping by the sides of the fields and fences. The cows which have young, in the meantime, forsake the flock and repair to the places where their calves are concealed, where, with flaming eyeballs and palpitating hearts, they seem resolved to maintain their ground at all hazards. The shooters always take care to avoid these retreats. When the object of pursuit is one of the older bulls of the flock, the shooting of it is a very hazardous employment. Some of these have been known to receive as many as eleven bullets, without one of them piercing their skulls. When fretted in this manner, they often become furious, and, owing to their great swiftness and prodigious strength, they are then regarded as objects of no ordinary dread. The White Urus, or Hamilton breed of wild cattle differs in many respects from any other known breed. As compared with those kept at Chillingham Park, Northumberland, by Lord Tankerville, they are larger, and more robust in the general form of their bodies, and their markings are also very different. In the Tankerville breed, the colour is invariably white, muzzle black, the whole of the inside of the ear, and about one-third of the outside, from the tip downwards, red. The horns are very fine, white, with black tips, and the head and legs are slender and elegant. In the Hamilton *urus* the body is dun-white, the inside of the ears, the muzzle, and the hoofs black, and the fore part of the leg, from the knee downwards, *mottled with black.* The cows seldom have horns ; their bodies are thick and short ; their limbs are stouter, and their heads much rounder than in the Tankerville breed. The inside or roof of the mouth is black or spotted with black. The tongue is black and generally tipped with black. It is somewhat larger in proportion than that of the common cow; and the high ridge on the upper surface, near to the insertion of the tongue, is also very prominent. It is observable that the calves that are of the usual markings are either entirely black or entirely white, or black and white, but never red or brown.

" The beef, like that of the Tankerville breed, is marbled, and of excellent flavour, and the juice is richer and of a lighter colour than in ordinary butcher-meat. The size of the smaller cows does not exceed fifteen stones tron weight ; but some of the larger sort, especially the bulls, average from thirty-five to forty-five stones. The circumstances of their breeding *in-and-in,* of being chased so much when any of them are to be shot, of being so frequently approached and disturbed by strangers, and of having been exposed so long to all the vicissitudes of the seasons, and constantly browsing the same pasture, have no doubt contributed greatly to the deterioration of the breed, and must have reduced them much in size and other qualities.

" The ancient history of this breed is involved in much mystery. From fossil remains, chiefly found in marl-pits, it appears that two species of the ox tribe formerly prevailed in Scotland, namely, the *Bos taurus* and the *Bos urus*. Some heads of these, of very large dimensions, are still preserved in the collections of the curious. Professor Fleming of Aberdeen informs us that he has a skull of the former in his possession, measuring $27\frac{1}{2}$ inches in length, 9 inches between the horns, and $11\frac{1}{2}$ inches across at the orbits. The accounts of ancient authors certainly allude to a species of wild cattle, very different in their character and dimensions from those of the present day. The favourite haunt of these animals in ancient times seems to have been the Caledonia Sylva, or Caledonian Forest, which extended from Stirling through Menteith and Stratherne, to Athol and Lochaber. It is described by old authors, as dividing the Picts from the Scots ; and, being well furnished with game, especially with fierce white bulls and kine, it was the place of both their huntings and of their greatest controversies. Some say it took its name from Calder which signifies a hazel, or common nutbush. The Roman historians delight much to talk of the furious white bulls which the Forest of Caledonia brought forth. In these early days they are represented as of large size, and as possessing *jubam densam, ac demissam instar leonis ;* or as Holinshed has it, crisp and curled manes like feirs leonis.

At what period this great forest was destroyed, and the white cattle extirpated is uncertain. Sir Robert Sibbald describes them in his time, as denuded of their manes. In the sixteenth century, they seem to have become entirely extinct as a wild race, and, as we learn from Gesner, were all slain except in that part which is called Cummernad. Another author informs us that thocht thir bullis were bred in sindry boundis of the Colidin Wod, now be continewal hunting and lust of insolent men, they are destroyit in all parts of

Scotland, and nane of them left but Allenerlie in
Cumernald. At what period the present breed
were introduced to the royal chase at Cadzow cannot
now be well ascertained. It is well known that the
Cummings were at one period proprietors of Cadzow
and Cumbernauld, and it is likely that in their time
the white cattle were in both places. But be that as
it may, they have long been extirpated at Cumbernauld; while they have been preserved in great
perfection at Hamilton. The universal tradition in
Clydesdale is that they have been at Cadzow from
the remotest antiquity; and the probability is, that
they are a part remaining of the establishment of our
ancient British and Scottish kings. At present they
are objects of great curiosity—both to the inhabitants
and to strangers visiting the place. During the
troubles consequent on the death of Charles I., and
the usurpation of Cromwell, they were nearly extirpated; but a breed of them having been retained for
the Hamilton family, by Hamilton Dalzell, and by
Lord Elphinstone at Cumbernauld—they were subsequently restored in their original purity. A
tradition prevails in the country, that, about
a hundred years ago, when it was found necessary for a time to remove them from one pasture
to another, several hundred individuals belonging to
the different baronies on the ducal estate were called
out, and that they only effected their purpose with
much difficulty and danger. Instances are recorded
of their having been taken when young and tamed,
and even milked. The milk, like that of most white
cattle, is described as thin and watery. The usual
number of ribs is thirteen on each side; some have
been slaughtered with fourteen pair of ribs, but this
is exceedingly rare. There is no other park of cattle
in Scotland of a similar description."

THE TOWN OF HAMILTON.

The town of Hamilton stands on a rising ground, gently sloping towards the east, about a mile west of the conflux of the Avon and the Clyde. Cadzow burn runs nearly through it. The ancient town stood farther to the east, in the Duke's pleasure grounds, and was called the Netherton. Mr Patrick says that part of the present town which stands near the flesh-market and the public green appears to be the most ancient. The rocks behind the flesh-market are about twenty feet high, and were once occupied by a mansion, called the Ha' or Hall, of which an antique dove-cot (which gives the name of doocot-ha' to the place) is the only memorial now remaining. On the opposite side of the burn stood a mill called the Ha' Mill, which has given the name of "Sheilling Hill" to the street where it stood. When the *tun, ton,* or town, collected round this place it was called Ha-mill-ton. So says tradition, but history, which is more to be depended on, gives, as we have already seen, a different and more satisfactory account. The date of the foundation of the lower part of the town cannot now be ascertained. It has been long swept away. That the upper part is also of great antiquity appears from the fact that it was considerable enough to be erected into a burgh of barony in the year 1456 by James II. In 1548, Hamilton was created a royal burgh by Queen Mary ; but Bailies James Hamilton and James Naismith consented to resign that privilege in 1670 by accepting of a charter from Duchess Anne, by which

5

Hamilton was constituted the chief burgh of the regality and dukedom of Hamilton. A law-suit was entered into by the magistrates, &c., in 1723, before the Court of Session, for the restoration of their ancient rights; but it was not till 1832 that the inhabitants were re-invested with the privilege of sending a member to the House of Commons. Hamilton is the capital of the Middle Ward of Lanarkshire, and is 10¾ miles S.E. of Glasgow, 36 W. of Edinburgh, 15 N.W. of Lanark, 7 N. of Strathaven, and 8 miles S. of Airdrie.

ECCLESIASTICAL HISTORY.

The ancient parish of Cadzow included the chapelry of Machan (the "little plain"), now the parish of Dalserf. The church with its pertinents was granted by David I., with consent of his son, Earl Henry, in perpetual alms to the church and bishops of Glasgow, and this grant was confirmed by the bulls of several Popes *inter* 1170 and 1186. Afterwards, with the lands of Barlanerk and Baldernock, it became the appropriate prebend of the Dean of the See of Glasgow. One of the rectors was William Frazer, who became Chancellor of Scotland. Another, in 1454, was Andrew Muirhead, a son of Muirhead of Lauchope, who became Bishop of Glasgow. The parish, by the influence of the first Lord Hamilton, was in 1454 made a collegiate charge, and a new edifice with a choir, two cross aisles, and a steeple— all of polished stone and highly ornamental—was erected. The patronage of this establishment was vested in Lord Hamilton, that of the parish church continuing as before with the Bishop of Glasgow. Manses, gardens, and glebes were provided for the Provost, and eight prebends, besides a manse, garden and glebe, for a chaplainry dedicated to the Virgin Mary. There is a farm at Eddlewood still called the Chapel. At the epoch of the Reformation, Mr Arch. Karry, "the vicar pensioner," had twenty merks yearly; and the Dean had £349 in money, 16 bolls of meal, 24 bolls of oats, and 24 capons yearly. The old collegiate church continued till 1732, and one of the cross aisles remained and was used as a burying-place by the Hamilton family prior to the completion of the noble mausoleum within the last thirty years.

By the Act establishing Presbyterianism as the national form of worship, two ministers were settled in Hamilton upon a provision of eighteen chalders of victual. Readers or catechists seem also to have existed. The former arrangement was not, however, lasting; for, though in 1590 Mr John Davidson is mentioned as first minister, and Mr Gavin Hamilton as second minister of Hamilton, there was only one minister for many years afterwards, with a stipend payable out of the deanery of Glasgow. Episcopacy took the place of Presbyterianism in 1606, and continued the Established faith—with brief interruption during Cromwell's rule—down to 1689, when Presbyterianism was fully restored. Mr Robert Wylie in 1692 became first minister, on the understanding that, as "formerly," he was to have a colleague. After a good deal of opposition, this arrangement was implemented in the appointment of Mr Alex. Findlator from Avondale.

TWO DISTINGUISHED ROMAN CATHOLIC RECTORS,

At the death of Alexander III, a distinguished man, William Frazer, was, as we have already noticed, rector of the parish. He afterwards became Lord Chancellor of Scotland and still later Bishop of St. Andrews. He was a guardian of the kingdom during the brief reign of Margaret the Maiden, but being a crafty self-seeking ambitious man, on the first rumour of the Queen's death, he sent an invitation to the English King to approach the Border. This was ostensibly to prevent bloodshed, but really to forward the Baliol interest of which he was a partisan. One of Rector Frazer's successors was, Alexander, fourth brother of Robert the Bruce. He espoused the cause of the Bruce, and was taken prisoner along with his brother, Thomas, while fighting against the M'Dowalls, a Galloway sept. His captors carried him to Carlisle, where, by order of the English King, he was hanged, his head being afterwards cut off and suspended at the gate of the merry border town.

REFORMATION ASSOCIATIONS—THE ATTITUDE OF THE HAMILTONS—JOHN KNOX.

The ties which knit the House of Hamilton and their burghers in feudal times had not lost any of their strength when the Reformation period dawned on Scotland. The head of the house was James, the second Earl of Arran and Duke of Chatelherault. He was of a vacillating and uncertain disposition, Popish and Protestant by turns, but neither long ; and the peoples' motto would appear to have been "like master like man." When he joined the Lords of the Congregation, he appointed Robert Hamilton of Bothwell—in the ancient church Rector of Torrens and prebendary of Bothwell—minister of the parish, and thus through his influence Hamilton was one of the few parishes that had from the first a regular pastor of the Reformed faith. Hamilton was the friend of John Knox and it is notable that of one of the Duke of Chatelherault's chaplains—Thomas Gwilliam, formerly a black friar—Calderwood relates " that he was the

first man from whome Mr Knox received ane taste
of the truthe." We need scarcely add that subsequent
to 1566 the Hamiltons lost favour with the Reformers
by supporting Queen Mary and her cause, and that
after the assassination of the Regent Moray by
Hamilton of Bothwell Haugh there was no language
too abusive or forcible that could be heaped upon them.

CHURCH DISCIPLINE 200 YEARS AGO.

About the year 1648, a Mr Naysmith was
appointed to the parish. He was a red-hot zealot for
Kirk and Covenant, and set himself to purge the
parish of its wickedness. After clearing his session
of certain adherents of Montrose, the worthy minister
set himself to deal with the prevalent immorality—
Sabbath-breaking, drinking, swearing, &c.—of the day.
His course of procedure will be best illustrated by
extracts from the records of kirk-session of the
period. One entry is—" The qlk day James Struthers
comperit and confest the breach of Sabbath, by
strykeing his neighbor, making that actioun his
daylie custome, and being censured, was ordained to
make his repentance in public place." Another—
" The qlk day ordains to summond Arthur Hamilton
in Merritoun for his absence from the church and
taking his barne to ane other church, the minister
being at home." A few days afterwards Arthur duly
appeared and promised never to be absent from church
in time coming, otherwise to be censured as a breaker
of the Sabbath. Arthur Hamilton of Auchingramont
was accused of kissing Isabell Granger betwixt the
doors on the Sabbath ; he denied the charge, and
witnesses were brought up against him on several
occasions. Finally, the following entry appears :—
" The qlk day comperit Arthur Hamilton of Auchingramont, and confest his misconduct with Isabell

Granger, . . . and thairfore being censured, was ordained to make his repentance in the public place." There was a good deal of bad feeling about Montrose in the parish. Here is an entry bearing on the subject—"The qlk day John Scott in Merritoun comperit and denyit that he sklanderit Patricke in saying that he did raise the people to ryde with James Grahame." There was a Jean Lang who had disobeyed the session, and been very refractory, and "the last of Appryll, 1646, the qlk day the Sessioun requests the baillies to take Jeane Lang and put her in the tolbuith till Satterday, and yrafter to put her on the cross, with ane paper upoune her heid." Besides Jean Lang, there were many other troublesome women in Hamilton, particularly of the name of Naysmith and Hamilton. "The qlk day Joane Naysmithe comperit and confest that she callet the people of God drytting puritans, was ordained to make her repentance in her awin seat." There was a great deal of drinking in Hamilton. Here is one of the Session's regulations on the subject—"The qlk day the Sessioun renewit their former act anent drinkers after ten of the clocke at night, and the baillies for that occasioun to cause ringe the ten hours bell at night." The following is a most excellent resolution: "The qlk day the Sessioun, taking to consideration the great prejudice to the gospell by selling of drink till men be drunken, thairfore the Sessioun ordains that quhosoever sells drink till men be drunken sal be punished with that same punishment that the druken man is punished with." Swearing also prevailed. The following is one of the entries on the subject:— "The qlk day the Sessioun, taking to their consideration the great disdaine done to the name of God by swearing, ordained that if any sall fall in the lyke sin, sall go to the publict place of repentance."

PREACHING AT THE GREAT DUKE.

Previous to setting out in command of the Forces sent to England to support King Charles I., the Duke of Hamilton attended church in Hamilton. The clergy were vehemently opposed to the expedition, and Mr Naysmith preached on the occasion, his text being Jeremiah xxii and 10—"Weep not ye for the dead, neither bemoan him ; but weep sore for him that goeth away, for he shall return no more." It is related that he used much freedom with the Duke in the course of his discourse, and pointedly applied the text to his Grace's case. The expedition, we need not add, ended in the defeat and capture of his Grace, who bravely suffered death in the following year.

Naysmith refused to take the oath of allegiance and was ejected from his living in 1662. Modifying his views a few years afterwards, he ended his life in 1674 as an "indulged" minister at Glasford.

PRESENT ECCLESIASTICAL CONDITION.

Past ecclesiastical divisions have multiplied the number of churches, but there is at the present time amongst the clergy of all denominations a pleasing absence of sectarian jealousy and bigotry. The parish church stands on a high ground adjoining Cadzow Street. The body of the church is a circle with four cross aisles. The design, which is generally accounted elegant, was by Adams, the elder. By decreet of modification and locality, dated 1st March, 1867, the stipend payable to the minister of the first charge is 182 bolls of meal, and 146 bolls, 1 peck and 2½ lippies of barley, Linlithgow measure, with £63 14s in money, including £10 for Communion elements. There was formerly a manse attached to the living, which was situated within what are now the policies of the Duke of Hamilton, and which was

acquired by his Grace, who, instead of building a new
manse, granted the then incumbent an annual allowance in name of house rent. This arrangement was
continued with successive ministers. During the
incumbency of the late Dr Keith the glebe was let to
the Duke ; and, for 15 years, the annual sum paid by
his Grace, as rent therefor, and in name of house
rent in lieu of manse, was £155. In 1875, the
mineral underneath the glebe was let to the Bent
Colliery Company (Limited) on lease for thirty years
from 1873. The rent, in the option of the lessors, is
a fixed sum of £300 per annum, or a lordship, and 10
per cent. of the annual produce is to be paid to the
incumbent for the time being, in respect of injury to
the amenity of the glebe, and personal inconvenience
and trouble, and the residue, after paying expenses,
is to be deposited in bank and invested for behoof of
the living. The Court of Teinds, on 13th March,
1876, granted power to the present incumbent to feu
the glebe, £20 per acre being fixed as the minimum
rate. The income of the minister, it is expected,
when the feuing, which has commenced, is completed,
will be increased by about £500 per annum, and this
would make the living one of the most desirable in
the Church. The feuing of the glebe necessitated
that the incumbent should get it into his own hands,
and that there should be a new arrangement with the
Duke of Hamilton in respect of allowance for a manse.
In the negotiations which followed, Mr Padwick, his
Grace's Commissioner, repudiated all obligation on
the part of the Duke to provide a manse and offices
or continue the annual money allowance therefor. Mr
Hamilton, the incumbent, acting on the advice of counsel,
thereupon called on the heritors to erect a manse and
make him a money allowance until this was done.
The request at once raised a question of no small

moment to the parishioners, as the assessment for defraying the cost of a manse would fall on the small feuars as well as upon the wealthy heritors, and this in all likelihood would raise an agitation which it was the interest of the friends of the Established Church to avoid. No solution of the difficulty has yet been arrived at. The committee of heritors, to whom it was referred, have, however, obtained an opinion of eminent counsel (the Lord-Advocate and Mr Lee, Sheriff of Perthshire) that the ultimate liability rests not upon the heritors but upon the Duke of Hamilton as representing his grandfather, and they suggest that the most expedient course is for the heritors to meet the minister's claim with an action of declarator directed against him and the Duke, concluding to have it found that the Duke is bound to erect a suitable manse and offices for the accommodation of the minister, and in any view that the heritors, if liable to furnish that accommodation in the first instance, are entitled to relief of their obligations at the hands of his Grace. It is to be hoped that the Duke's advisers will see their way to withdraw from the position they have taken up. The minister of the second charge has a manse but no glebe. His stipend is understood to yield £500 annually. Auchingramont Church, a handsome Gothic edifice, was erected about eighteen years ago, the accommodation in the Parish Church having been for long insufficient. The first and second ministers conduct the services in both churches, preaching alternately forenoon and afternoon. Two years ago, Cadzow Church was erected at Woodside Walk, and its endowment is being carried through the Court of Teinds. In connection with the National Church there is an unendowed chapel at Quarter, and mission agencies at Burnbank and elsewhere.

Non-conformity, from an early period, played an important part in the ecclesiastical polity of the parish. The Blackswell U.P. congregation, now worshipping in Saffronhall Church, dates back to 1755. Twenty-one years later, in the spring of 1776, the second charge of the parish being vacant, a large body of parishioners to whom the presentee was unacceptable, formed the Relief Church, and built the place of worship in Muir street, now used as a volunteer store, and which was evacuated upon the congregation removing to the new and elegant structure now occupied by them in Auchingramont Road. The Chapel Street United Presbyterian Congregation was founded about the end of last century, and the Brandon Street congregation—a split off Muir Street—in 1831. A new church in Duke Street was erected in 1835 in connection with the Establishment, which, since the Disruption, has been the leading—indeed, until a few years ago, when a church was built at Burnbank Road —the only Free Church in Hamilton. Besides these there is a Congregational Church in Auchingramont Road, which was formed in a building in Blackswell about seventy years ago; an Episcopalian Church in the same thoroughfare ; an Evangelical Union Chapel in Park Road ; a Roman Catholic Chapel in Cadzow Street, formed in 1846. At Burnbank, a neat and commodious wooden structure has been built for the United Presbyterian Mission to the mining population of that quarter. There is a missionary labouring in the same district in connection with the Free Church.

MARTYRS OF THE COVENANT.

Hamilton has in precious keeping dust of martyrs of the Covenant. Into the east wall of the Church-yard, there is built a monument, which, from its grotesque appearance, is one of the first objects to arrest the eye of the visitor on entering the enclosure. It is a slab of freestone, four feet two inches in length, by two feet eight inches in breath. It has the following inscription :—

AT HAMILTON
LIE THE HEADS OF
JOHN PARKER, GAVIN HAMILTON,
JAMES HAMILTON,
AND
CHRISTOPHER STRANG,
WHO SUFFERED AT
EDINBURGH,
DEC. 7TH 1666.

FOUR HEADS IN BASSO-RELIEVO.

Stay, passenger, take notice
what thou reads.
At Edinburgh lie our bodies,
here our heads.
Cur right hands stood at Lanark,
these we want,
Because with them we sware
the Covenant.

Renewed
MDCCCXXVIII.

The four heads in basso-relievo are sculptured in the rudest manner. Indeed (says the Rev. Mr Thomson in his "Martyr Graves of Scotland"), so grotesquely criminal are the features, that they look like the work of an enemy rather than a friend.

John Parker was a waulker, *i. e.*, a fuller of cloth in East Kilbride; Gavin Hamilton, a tenant in Carluke; James Hamilton, a tenant in Killiemuir; and Christopher Strang, tenant in East Kilbride. All four were taken prisoners at Pentland. They were tried at Edinburgh before the Council. Sharp was president, and with his native ferocity, urged on

their condemnation. It was pleaded on their behalf
that since quarter had been given them by such as
had the king's commission to kill or save, and Grotius,
in those days the great authority upon such matters,
had, in his treatise, "De Jure Belli et Pacis," determined
that "faith is to be kept even with rebels," they could
not be put to death. But Sharp secured that this
pleading be put aside, and that the trial take place.
It is said that even Dalziel, bloodthirsty as he un-
doubtedly was, when he heard of this pressing on of
the trial, cursed and swore terribly, and declared were
he to serve the king ever so long, he should never
bring in a prisoner to be butchered. The record of
the trial is given at length in Wodrow, book II. c. i. s.,
3. Its replies, its duplies, its triplies, and quadruplies,
are interesting as a specimen of the mode of procedure
in a Scotch Court in the seventeenth century—a mode
of procedure which actually continued to the beginning of this century—as well as for their able reason-
ing. The advocates for the prisoners seem to have
done what they could in their defence ; but all was of
no avail. They were sentenced to be hanged at Edinburgh on the next Friday, December 7th, 1666 ; and
after they were dead, their heads " to be cut off," and
"affixed at Hamilton" ; and "their right hands on the
" public ports " of Lanark, " being the place where
they took the Covenant." " Naphtali " contains the
" Joint Testimony " of the four and other six con-
demned along with them, a second testimony, and
three other individual testimonies. The close of the
first testimony is remarkable for its confidence in the
ultimate triumph of the cause for which they suffered
and died. It is :

" And further, we are assured, though this be the
day of Jacob's trouble, that yet the Lord when He
hath accomplished the trial of His own, and filled up

the cup of His adversaries, He will awake for judgment, plead his own cause, avenge the quarrel of His Covenant, make inquiry for blood, vindicate His people, break the arm of the wicked, and establish the just ; for to Him belongeth judgment and vengeance, and though our eyes shall not see it, yet we believe that the sun of righteousness shall arise with healing under his wings ; and that He will revive His work, repair the breaches, build the old wastes, and raise up the desolations ; yea, the Lord will judge His people, and repent Himself for His servants, when their power is gone, and there is none shut up or left. And therefore, rejoice, O ye nations, with His people ; for He will avenge the blood of His servants, and will render vengeance to His adversaries, and He will be merciful to His land and people. So, let thy enemies perish, O Lord ! but let them that love Him be as the sun when he goeth forth in his might."

Mr Dodds has ferreted out, in the State Paper Office, a letter from Main, the postmaster in Edinburgh, to the Government in London, giving an account of their death. "All of them died adhering to the Covenant, declaring they never intended in the least any rebellion, and all of them prayed most earnestly for his majesty's interest, and against his enemies." "They prayed to forgive the judges and the noblemen, and declared their blood lay only at the prelate's door—would not be hindered to express themselves in such a manner—which expressions had too great dipping in the hearts of the commonality."

EDUCATIONAL.

Hamilton, from remote to present times, has been unusually well served educationally. The grammar school is of ancient date. In 1588, we find Lord

John Hamilton granting a bond, still in possession of
the corporation, settling for ever on that school the
yearly sum of 20 pounds Scots. In the old school-
house, which still stands, and which gives the name
to a spacious square in the old town, Pillans, Whale,
Gillies, and other eminent men taught; James, Duke
of Hamilton, grandson of the good Duchess Anne,
received part of his education, as did Dr William
Cullen, Dr M. Baillie, Professor Miller, Lord Dundonald; and there were sent from it pupils who, in
the town and spheres far beyond, have made their
mark, and are even now sustaining well their part in
the world. The old grammar school, in its time, did
much for the cause of secondary education in the
district. In 1847, new premises were erected on a
commanding site near the Leechlee, and opened under
the name of the Academy. It included the parish
school, and represented the old grammar school.
The teaching staff more than sustained the high
character inherited from the older institution. When,
on the passing of Lord Young's Education Act, the
School Board was brought into existence, the
Academy was the only existing school which passed
under the Board. Being in a most prosperous condition, the future of the institution became a source
of anxiety to the members of the School Board. It
taught many branches besides the elementary; and
the scale of fees charged deprived it of assistance
from the grant. It had always been essentially a
higher-class school in the sense of the Act, and the
Scotch Education Department so designated it after
considering the flattering report of the inspector who
reported on it. It was so in the estimation of the
Board, who, after long deliberation, resolved, in terms
of the statute, that it should be so regarded, and that
the Board of Education should be asked to sanction

its being so enrolled and treated. This resolution was the result of very much and anxious thought to the Board, who deprecated the possibility of the status of the School being lowered, and also considered that, for the sake of the town and district, it should be ranked as a high-class school. In their resolution on the subject, the Board redeemed a pledge which they gave to the parish Board—that, in respect of the latter Board foregoing their claim to the parochial part of the Academy, the Board should do what they could to have the Academy ranked as a higher-class school. The want of any endowment, which was the great obstacle in the way, was eventually overcome, and the Academy, still under its able head (Mr Blacklock), but equipped with an almost entirely new staff of highly-trained teachers, began the session of 1876-77 as a higher-class school. The success attending it has been most gratifying, and has evidently not yet reached the highest point. Last session, its examiners were Mr Andrews and Mr Smith, the Government inspectors of the district. They conducted the examination, not in virtue of their official position, but at the invitation of the School Board. Their ability and perfect impartiality are, therefore, beyond question, and Mr Andrews concluded a highly flattering report in the following terms :—

"I would conclude my report in remarking that what impressed me as the leading feature of the school, a feature running through all its departments, and down into the minutest detail of its working, was the thoroughness with which everything attempted was gone into, the downright honesty and soundness of all the teaching, and the utter absence of anything like educational quackery or sham. Healthy vigour and genuine work pervade its whole atmosphere, and as, under the fostering care of the School Board, it gradually widens its aims, and reaches up to higher levels of study, I have no doubt that the Hamilton Academy will come to occupy a leading position among the secondary schools of the country."

St. John's Grammar School, conducted by Mr
Adams and an efficient staff of masters, has been an
incalculable blessing to the town. Conducted with
unflagging energy and zeal—teaching at a moderate
rate the higher as well as elementary branches—its
pupils are to be found in every walk of life, many of
them adorning the professions. The Quarry School,
under the Orphan and Charity Society, and St. Mary's
School, in connection with the Roman Catholic
Church, impart instruction of excellent quality to the
very poorest class in the community. There are two
elementary schools under the management of the
School Board, which are faithfully doing their work.
When the Board was brought into existence six years
ago, the number of children between five and thirteen
years of age was found to be 2,211, and of these 824
were not attending school. There was a deficiency
of school accommodation for 1062 children, and
allowing for the opening of schools in suitable districts
by the Parish Board, the Board resolved to provide
accommodation for 750. To meet this, they erected
a building in Beckford Street to accommodate 350,
and another at Townhead Street for 400. Beckford
Street School was opened in August, and Townhead
School in November, 1875. Under the management
of the Parish Board, there are schools at Greenfield,
Low-waters, Motherwell, Quarter, Beechfield, and
Ferniegair.

Of private establishments, the Clydesdale College is
efficiently conducted by Messrs Wood and Kinmond.
Miss Neilson, in Clydesdale Street, and the Misses
Spence, at Earnock View, have establishments for
young ladies.

MUNICIPAL.

From 1832, down to the present year, the town was
governed by a Provost, three bailies, a treasurer, a

town clerk, and seven councillors. The town latterly was divided into four wards, and a representative of each retired annually. The gas works, having been acquired from a private company, are managed by the Town Council, and are in course of being greatly extended. The water works, from their erection, until the November of this year, were managed by a body of Commissioners. From time to time the state of the old town forced the question of improvements into prominence, and application to Parliament was long talked of. Some of the worst evils connected with the old town disappeared before the rapid increase of workmen's houses, which, prompted by high rents, private enterprise was providing in other and better parts of the town, and the need for an Improvement Bill was becoming less and less urgent when new causes for going to Parliament presented themselves. The Water Commissioners, though they had been in Parliament so recently as 1875 for borrowing and other powers, were again requiring money to bring the abundant supply of water which they had collected at the ponds at Townhead down to the town. There was scarcity in the high-lying parts of the burgh, and the new suburbs at Burnbank and Greenfield were calling out for a supply. These suburbs had almost sprung up in a night, and were the direct result of the opening up of the coalfields in that direction, stimulated by the speculation mania which had just spent itself in Glasgow, and which settled here after for a time casting about for fresh fields. These suburbs not only wanted water and gas, but they required drainage, and streets to be formed, &c. They applied to be taken into the municipality, and were refused, and they then asked the Sheriff to form them into a burgh under the Police Act. The Town Council, with the prospect of having a divided jurisdiction so near their borders, and requiring to go to Parliament for water purposes at any rate, after taking a plebiscite of the inhabitants—with whom it was distinctly stipulated that the benefits of the common good should not extend beyond the old boundaries— resolved to make application for a Bill for the extension and improvement of the burgh. The Bill was determinedly opposed in both Houses of Parliament, but ultimately passed, and with it greater and more important changes have been brought · about than since the Reform Act of 1832. The portion annexed, including Burnbank, Greenfield, and Low-waters, is constituted the Fifth Ward of the burgh, with three representatives in the Town Council, which is thus increased to fifteen members. A fourth bailie is added to the magistracy, who is to be Dean of Guild. The Dean's Court consists of a Depute-Dean and three Councillors, and enlarged powers are conferred upon it. The Water Commissioners ceased to exist on 11th November, 1878, and the management of the works passed into the hands of the Town Council. Power is also given to elect a Chamberlain, who is not to be a member of Town Council, and to carry out several important improvement works.

Hamilton unites with Falkirk, which is the returning burgh, Lanark, Linlithgow, and Airdrie, in sending a member to Parliament. The constituency for 1878-79 numbers 1292, the part recently annexed being, so far as Parliamentary representation is concerned, still in the county. The population of the burgh in 1871 was 11,496 ; the present population (inclusive of the extended portion) is estimated at about 17,000. The total valuation for 1878-79 of the old and extended burgh, including railways, is set down at £77,297 13s.

The following names appear in the minutes of Council, being those of Provosts or Chief Magistrates and Bailies:—From 1735 to 1787—J. Porterfield, James Semple, Wm. Cullen, Thos. Cunison, Quintin Hamilton, Thomas Duning, William Mather, John Naismith, John Aitton, James Syme, John Bryson, James Hamilton, George Wands, Wm. Brown; from 1801 till the present time—John Hinshaw, John Torrance, James Haldane, Will. Hamilton, James Henderson, Robert Henderson, Thomas Anderson, James Naismith, Walter Black, Alexander Gibson, John Meek, Robert Henderson, James Nisbet, John Dykes, W. A. Dykes, John Clark Forrest.

BURGH REVENUE.

The Town's Lands were acquired from James, Lord Hamilton, by charter, dated 14th October, 1474, and they are also contained in a charter by Anne, Duchess of Hamilton, with consent of William, Duke of Hamilton, her husband, dated the 1st day of June, 1670. No part of these lands, so far as known, has been alienated by the town since the date of acquiring them, except the ground feued out for an annual feu-duty, and certain small parts given in exchange as after-mentioned.

By disposition granted by Anne, Duchess of Hamilton, dated 22d August, 1695, she, in lieu of an acre of the Muir of the Burgh, which had been imparked with her Laigh Park, disponed to the town an acre of her field land, next to the east side of the Muir of Hamilton; and in this acre, with the teinds thereof, the Magistrates and Council were infeft conform to instrument of sasine, dated 11th, and registered 12th September, 1695. The acre of ground thus disponed, comprehends those feus belonging to the town on the east side of Muir Street.

By the disposition last mentioned, Duchess Anne also dispones in excambion of the old common green of the burgh, all and haill, these homes and haill ground betwixt the burn of Hamilton and the lade that leads the water to the mill thereof from the Mill-dam-back down to the Shealing-hill. The town also acquired, in lieu of the old green, for a price paid by Duchess Anne, from James Lowdon, litstor in Hamilton, all and whole that acre of land called Ducot acre, lying on the south side of the wynd called St John's Wynd or Muir Wynd, and on the west side of the yard called Ducot-hall Yard, conform to disposition dated 22d August, 1695, and in which the Magistrates and Council were infeft conform to instrument of sasine, dated the 11th, and recorded on the 12th day of September, 1695, and which writs are confirmed by charter from Duchess Anne, dated 22d September, 1695.

This acre, with the holms and ground above-mentioned, and certain parts of the lands of Rogerscroft, feued by the town from the heirs of Archibald Weir, and from John Campbell of Saffronhall, form the present common bleaching green of the burgh.

No part of these has been alienated by the town except those parts feued out to the late Mr George Wands and Dr Wharrie, and a small part to the Relief Congregation. The extent of the present bleaching green and holms is 2 acres 1 rood and 24 falls.

By agreement entered into between the Magistrates and Council and the Duke of Hamilton, dated in October, 1829, His Grace discharged certain arrears of feu and teind duties due by the town, with the valued price of the teinds, for which decree of sale was obtained on 3d July, 1799, the whole amounting to £453 12s 6d sterling. The town has now right to the teinds of these lands, but no regular disposition to the same has been yet obtained.

The Council house tenement was acquired by disposition from Duchess Anne, dated 3d August, 1707, and in which the town was infeft, conform to instrument of sasine dated 16th September, and recorded 2d October, 1707. The old Flesh-market of the burgh formerly occupied the site of this tenement. The present tenement was built in the year 1796.

The Meal Market tenement was acquired by the town by disposition from John Muir, maltman in Hamilton, and in which the town was infeft conform to instrument of sasine, dated 17th and recorded 19th June, 1699. The titles of the town are confirmed by the superior conform to confirmation dated 14th July, 1713.

The Grammar School and rector's house were acquired by disposition from Duchess Anne, dated 15th February, 1714, and instrument of sasine following thereon in favour of the town, dated the same day, and recorded 18th February, 1714.

The site of the present fleshmarket and slaughterhouse and adjoining ground was acquired from the doers of the deceased Douglas, Duke of Hamilton and Brandon, in exchange for a small piece of ground lying next the gate to the entry to Hamilton Palace, at Gallowhill. The agreement was settled by missives, dated 6th February, 1784, and both parties have since possessed the respective pieces of ground got in exchange. The transaction was completed by a regular contract of excambion. The town stands infeft, conform to instrument of sasine, dated 2d, recorded 11th June, 1829. The present fleshmarket and slaughter-house were erected in 1794.

That derived from mineral is now by far the largest

item of revenue. Despite gloomy presages to the contrary, we hope the coal may realise the large expectations formed of it: the benefit to the town will be great and obvious, as taxation will not only be remitted, but the Town Council will be furnished with the means to carry out many useful improvements. In Treasurer Mackie's financial statement for the year ending 15th October, 1878, the land and mineral rents are shown to have amounted to £2765 18s 9d, making a total from this source, since the coal began to be worked, of £3140 12s 4d. During the year in question, there was derived from feu-duties, £1023 1s 6½d; from house rents, £246 5s 4d; town hall, £156 9s; and the miscellaneous revenue was £174 11s 6d. Few towns in Scotland are fortunate enough to possess such a valuable common good.

CHARITIES.

I. Robertson's mortification, or what is called the town's hospital. James Robertson, sheriff-clerk of Lanarkshire by deed of mortification, dated 4th Sept., 1657, disponed the lands of Airdrie, Rawyards, and Arbuckles, in the parish of New Monkland, to the magistrates and town council, and to the ministers and kirk session of the parish of Hamilton; and bequeathed certain moveable funds for the purpose of endowing an hospital. The deed was reduced as far as regards the heritage by Mr Robertson's heir-at-law. The moveable funds, with the addition of a sum bequeathed for a similar purpose by a Mr Lyon, came into the hands of the town, and yield £38 yearly, which is paid to nine old men, who receive £4 each— £2 of salary being paid to a factor. The hospital is under the management of the magistrates and town council and ministers and kirk session. They nominate alternately.

II. Mr John Rae, Mr Hamilton of Floors, and Miss Mary Mathie, severally mortified funds to the town, yielding £9 12s 4d, to be paid to poor persons. It is distributed yearly, according to a list made up by the magistrates and council.

III. Anne, Duchess of Hamilton, mortified one hundred pounds to the kirk session of the parish, for behoof of certain schools in the parish.

IV. Mr Michael Naismith mortified £100 to the town ; the interest of which was to be applied in educating twelve poor children. The children on this mortification are nominated by the magistrates and Council, or rather they appoint one of their members, who sees that the number of children is full. (The Hamilton Orphan Society also educate about 70 children yearly.)

V. Aikman of Ross burdened his lands of Burn-house with a fund for endowing an hospital in Hamilton. A house was accordingly built for the accommodation of four old men. They are elected alternately by the proprietor of Ross, the ministers of the parish, and the magistrates of the burgh, who are managers of the hospital. Besides a house, the old men receive each £5 yearly, with a hat and pair of shoes, and a suit of clothes every second year.

VI. Mr John Roxburgh of Bothwell Shields, burdened certain parts of his property with £10 10s yearly, to be paid to poor inhabitants of the town. The managers are—the eldest bailie of Hamilton, and certain of Mr Roxburgh's relations. The money is drawn and distributed yearly among poor persons, according to a list made up by the managers.

VII. Major Burns, in 1844 or 1845, mortified to the town the sum of £500, the interest of which was to be paid to three aged persons. The magistrates, council, and ministers of the parish, and certain trustees, are joint patrons.

VIII. Mrs Andrew Simpson, Haddow Street, Hamilton, in 1867 mortified £803 3s 2d, yielding £40 yearly, to be paid to poor persons belonging to the town of Hamilton. Ten old females receive £4 each yearly, and are appointed by the Town Council.

PUBLIC BUILDINGS—THE TOWN HALL.

The architectural character of the public buildings has made great advances. The new Town Hall was opened in 1863. It occupies the south-east corner site at the intersection of Duke and Quarry Streets. The style adopted by the architects (Messrs Clarke & Bell, Glasgow) is that of modernised Scotch baronial. The facade to Duke Street, though plain, is extremely fine, but the most prominent object of the building is the tower which stands at the corner of Duke and Quarry Streets, and which rears its tall and beautiful form to a height of nearly 130 feet. On the basement floor are situated the town clerk's office, police court, office, cells, &c. A stair leads from the principal public entrance in the tower to the Council Chambers and large hall, which is 63 feet long by 36 feet wide, and capable of accommodating from 400 to 500. The hall is fitted with a splendid organ, a public memorial to the late esteemed Provost John Dykes. There are ample retiring accommodation, and a commodious lesser hall 29 feet by 19 feet.

The Corporation, eighteen months since, acquired, at considerable outlay, a site near Gateside for new municipal buildings, the erection of which has not, however, yet been resolved upon.

THE OLD TOLBOOTH.

The old jail, now within His Grace's policies, was

built in the reign of Charles I. In its front balcony stood many a culprit as a spectacle to the gaping crowd. Strange associations are connected with this ancient structure, and stranger still the many scenes which have been enacted within its walls. Restrictions in feasting and drinking were winked at in those days. It was not unusual to see the bottle handed out and in at pleasure, and if the funds permitted, the debtor might drink his fill without let or hindrance. There were then no first, second, or third rate diets, no special wards, no turnkeys, save one ; no cranks, no oakum-picking, or hard labour. The jailer himself was a hearty " old buck," occupying a shop underneath the belfry and the bell, where he could see all that was going on. Jokes, toasts, songs, jigs, were the rule, and grief or *ennui* the exception. It is reported that on one occasion the jailer allowed a prisoner his freedom for a few hours to attend the funeral of a relative. Not very far from the prison, another place had the endearing appellation of the "Deil's Elbow," and further down was the "Back Burn." In the building opposite there still stands what was once the town hall, where feasting and drinking were carried on at the public expense. Whisky was then cheap and stomachs strong. Francis Wakefield knew this when he presented the Town Council with the capacious punch bowl still so much prized.

THE COUNTY BUILDINGS.

At a period comparatively remote, the Sheriff-Court business in the Lower Ward of Lanarkshire was of so little importance that it was all taken to Hamilton, which was then the seat of the Court for the Lower Ward, including the City of Glasgow, as well as for the whole of the Middle Ward. The late Sheriff Aiton was wont to tell that within his recol-

lection the office of Sheriff-Substitute was filled by a
weaver, and his salary was only £30. " During his
time," says the Sheriff, " I learned from my fellow
practitioners (two of whom had been doing business
in the Court for more than 50 years prior to 1798)
the practice was to hold the Court in a public-house
kept by a tailor, who was then head sheriff-clerk, and
in these patriarchal days the Judge was employed in
making and distributing the toddy amongst the practitioners and their clients whilst the business of the
Court was going on. The ordinary routine of a
process was then as it continued to be for many years
afterwards : (1) summons or petition ; (2) defences;
(3) answers ; (4) replies ; and (5) sometimes duplies.
I have seen an original process in which all these
pleadings were written on a single sheet of paper, and
the sum charged for drawing and extending seemed
to be 2s 6d for each. If the parties and procurators
had been so disposed and the bench not too potent,
all these pleadings might have been written and
interchanged, and the whole process ready for
decision at a single sitting. Later, the practice was
to write long papers. On one occasion, when there
was laid on the Court table an action of damages
against the owner of a hen that had strayed into a
bowl shop and broken some coarse crockery, one of
the octogenarians referred to, after looking at the
number and size of the papers which had been prepared by young practitioners who wanted to show off,
held up his hands and exclaimed in the way of
soliloquy—' All that about a hen ; what if it had
been a cow ?' And on another occasion, when a
short defence had been made with a very long
answer, the old-fashioned agent told his client in a
voice shaking with astonishment and consternation,
that the opposite agent had given in a paper as thick

as ——, and after looking round and groping with both hands for a suitable simile, he gave up the attempt in despair, and filled up the hiatus with the words, 'as thick as his head,' meaning them to be taken in their literal sense, and never dreaming that they could admit of any other interpretation." It is needless to say what a different state of things now exist. There have been established courts at Glasgow and Airdrie, and yet the business before the Hamilton Court is one of the largest in the county. It has advanced with the onward march of commerce and population in the district. This was well illustrated by Sheriff Spens in taking leave of the bar on his removal to Glasgow in December 1876. His Lordship said that when he took his seat on the bench in 1870, the population of the district was between 70,000 and 80,000. Since then it had increased in a marvellously rapid way, and he believed now the population could not be less than nearly 110,000. The reason of this was partially, or rather, he should say, chiefly, due to the immense impetus given to coal and iron development by the abnormal prices and demand during the years 1872, 1873, and 1874. With the increase of the population, there had been an increase in the work of the Court. In the year 1870 there were 1063 Small Debt cases in Wishaw and Hamilton, 103 Debts' Recovery cases, and 104 cases on the Ordinary roll. In 1875, although the Wages' Arrestment Act was in force, the number of Small Debt cases had risen to 1630 ; Debts' Recovery cases, 199 ; Ordinary cases, 279. The increase has been going on steadily every year since.

The buildings were begun in 1834, and have since been altered and enlarged. Their Grecian aspect and pillared facade and pediment are calculated to favourably impress strangers, but internally the accommodation is quite inadequate, and the ventilation, drainage, and general sanitary condition, of the worst description. The officials, practitioners, and Court-house Commissioners have each made representations on the subject to the Government, who have caused an inspection to be made, but nothing further has yet been done.

THE PRISON.

The prison is situated behind the Court-house. The two buildings were erected together in 1834-35 at an outlay of £7000—the half of which may be considered the cost of the prison. The population of the burgh was then between seven and eight thousand. A few years afterwards the cells were reduced in number, but increased in size and improved in ventilation ; and, at the same time, a bath-room, wash-house, and six stone-breaking sheds were erected, and half an acre of additional ground acquired to provide for future requirements—all at an additional cost of about £1000. The accommodation of the prison has never been sufficient, and in 1873, when trade was good and Hamilton becoming the centre of a large working population, it was evident that a considerable extension would require to be made. The Prison Board took up the question, and, after mature deliberation, finally, in 1876, approved of a plan which would have provided accommodation for the whole of the southern district of Lanarkshire, leaving the prisons of Airdrie and Lanark in their existing state for the detention of short-sentenced prisoners. When this plan was submitted to the authorities in Edinburgh it was rejected, as the Government had then a legislative measure in contemplation, which was shortly afterwards introduced into Parliament, though not passed into law until the following session. This Act, which applied to the whole country, came into force on 1st April, 1878. Under its provisions the Prison Board was abolished, and the entire prison adminis- tration vested in the Home Office, with a Depart- ment in Edinburgh controlling the management of the Scotch Prisons. It is believed that a new prison will ultimately be erected at Hamilton for the southern district of the county.

MILITARY.

The Barracks in Almada Street cover a large area, which is surrounded by a high wall. The cavalry element formerly predominated, but the erection of the Maryhill Barracks, and changed ideas at head- quarters led, much to the regret of the inhabitants, to the withdrawal of the horse soldiers in the summer of 1877. Under Lord Caldwell's Army Organisation scheme, Hamilton was selected as a double depot, and was constituted the 59th and 60th sub-districts, the regiments linked in the former being the 26th (Cameronians) and 74th (Highlanders), and in the latter the 73d and 90th. For the accommodation of the foot soldiers, the horse barracks have been utilized; also the buildings formerly the stores of the 1st Royal Lanark Militia ; and fine new quarters for officers and men built, and the hospital greatly enlarged. The head-quarters of the 1st Royal Lanark Militia are at Hamilton, and the barracks and erections connected therewith adjoin those of the Regulars. The Queen's Own Yeomanry meet annually for training in Hamilton, finishing up their week's drill with a review and races. The head- quarters of the 16th Lanarkshire Rifle Volunteers are also here.

POORHOUSE AND HOSPITAL.

There is a commodious poorhouse in Bothwell Road for the accommodation of paupers belonging to the parish, and to the adjoining parishes of Dalserf, Stonehouse, Glassford, Avondale, Cambuslang, Blantyre, and East Kilbride. The parish and burgh local authorities have joined in the erection of a fever hospital in Beckford Street, which is just approaching completion. It will be utilized for accident and other emergency cases.

RAILWAYS.

Through the influence of the ducal family, the Caledonian main line was diverted from Hamilton, which continued up till 1876 to be indifferently served by a branch line from South Side, Glasgow, with a terminus at Clydesdale Street. There was a 'bus required for conveyance from the railway station to the centre of Hamilton on the one hand, and to the centre of Glasgow on the other. After a severe struggle in Parliament, the Caledonian Railway Company obtained powers to construct a line connecting their terminus in Clydesdale Street with the Lesmahagow Railway, and an independent company, a railway from the North British system at Shettleston to Hamilton by way of Uddingston and Bothwell. By the one, the district to the south of Holytown and in the Lesmahagow direction are brought within easy access, and by the other a most interesting country is opened up and passengers set down in the centre of Glasgow. The Caledonian stations are at Quarry Street and Clydesdale Street; those of the Glasgow, Bothwell, Hamilton, and Coatbridge Railway in Cadzow Street and adjoining Peacock Cross. For unequalled facilities and cheapness, Hamilton, as regards travelling, would probably rank with the most highly-favoured town in the Kingdom.

RETROSPECTIVE.

To hark back for a brief space to those days, a few generations ago, when life was more simple and homely than it is now, the condition of the burgh, as illustrated by the public records of the time, may justly claim passing reference. Take the epoch of the Rebellion, or one hundred and forty years ago. The Palace was in the centre of the town, and its noble possessor knew everybody and everybody knew him. It is said of an old woman that she was in the habit of exulting over the fact that she "lived next door to the Duke," and that His Grace often called on her for a "light of his pipe." Upwards from the old Tolbooth, towards the west and south, there stretched the Castle Wynd, the New or School Wynd, and the Muir Wynd. Along this last road, from the Dovecothall and manse upwards, in the Bothwell direction, there seem to have been no houses, except, perhaps, one on the Muirbrow at Saffronhall, belonging to Mr Campbell; and through the wilderness of whins which overspread the Muir, both below that house and beyond it, there led the rough, narrow old road to Bothwell Bridge, along which many then living remembered to have met the fugitives from the famous battle, as after the fighting and the preaching of that eventful day they fled from Monmouth's army and the revengeful pursuit of Claver's dragoons. Branching off the road to Bothwell Bridge, there seems to have been a track through the whins nearly in the line of what is now Almada Street and Burnbank Road, and in 1736 there was the first attempt to make this track into something like a road for foot passengers and horses. By order of Town Council it was to be a "road or casway of an elne wide," or if Jackson of Bardykes, the laird of Westburn, and other proprietors in that direction subscribed liberally,

the Bailies and Council promised to extend the width
to four feet. At the head of the School Wynd, near
the mill and the miller's house, and beside the
Shieling Hill, the Grammar School then stood alone,
and past it there led a path to the then new kirk. In
1751, the Duke feued the ground west of the
Grammar School, and in the same year the first
houses in the Church Road were built by James
Bishop and others. At an early period the Duke's
almshouse was set down at the Old Cross; and the
Grammar School Square, under the name of the
Hawk Hill, was the place where the noble family
kept their falcons. At a later period a Quaker's
burying-ground was laid out exactly at the place
where the Edinburgh Road enters Hamilton. There
was the Castle Wynd Port, and near it, projecting
awkwardly into the street, an open draw well. It
cost the Council much labour to get led away and
down the Blackswell the water from Woodside and
Quarryloan, which had a perverse but not unnatural
inclination to run down the Castle Wynd and
" damnify the casway," as the minutes tell us. The
houses did not extend far up the Quarryloan, but
they were to be found in straggling fashion along
Townhead and out towards Broken Cross. Away
east and north from the old Tolbooth across the
haugh there were several roads and streets of which
there is now no trace. There was the Netherton
Wynd leading northward to the Muir Wynd; the
High Street or Hie Town, leading eastwards from the
Tolbooth towards the old front of the Palace; the
Langloan branching southwards from this towards
Huttonbank, and crossing the road to the Ross, and
there was the causeway leading to the Boathouse and
the boats. The Boathouse was at the mouth of the
Hamilton Burn; and, at the junction of the burn

with the Clyde, a quay was formed where lay two boats, one for cattle and carriages, which in those days were rare, and a little one for passengers. The boathouse and boats were let for a considerable period of time to some worthy man or woman, who took the management and drew the "customs" for the ferry.

THE COUNCIL AND THE FERRY FOLKS.

Very kind, says the late Provost John Dykes, the bailies and Council always were to the ferry folks, especially when Isobel Naismith was the tackswoman, and she held the ferry for a good many years. When Isobel's chimney smoked the treasurer had to see about it; and when, by reason of the long frost, the people crossed on the ice, to her great loss and detriment, she got, as was reasonable, an allowance out of her rent; and when there was a long drought, and they forded the water, her case was considered; and on all occasions the repair of her house and her personal comfort were looked after with a care and liberality which speaks volumes for the gallantry of the bailies towards the lone woman at the ferry. It was after her time, however, that the greatest misfortunes of any befel the boats. On the 11th of November, 1760, by "an extraordinary great flood in the water of Clyde," as the minutes tell us, "the large boat was so much shattered and broken that it could not be mended, and so must be made of new, without which there could be no passage in the winter season for horses and heavy carriages." Seven years afterwards the boats were both carried away by the ice; and altogether it must have been a great relief to the town when in 1780 the New Bridge, as it is still called, was opened, and the boats

7

were sold off by public roup. The customs for the boats, as fixed in 1761, in sterling money, were as follows :—

Each foot passenger, a halfpenny stg.   ...   ... $\frac{1}{2}$d.
Each horse or cow, one penny   ...   .   1d.
Each loaden single cart, fourpence ...   .   4d.
Each unloaden single cart, twopence   ...   ...   2d.
Each double loaden cart, eightpence   ...   ...   8d.
Each fourwheel chaise with 2 horses, eightpence,   8d.
Each fourwheel chaise, with 4 horses, one shilling
    fourpence ...   .   1s 4d.
Each coach with six horses, two shillings...   ...   2s
Each single horse load that requires to be un-
    loaded on boating, one penny, besides the
    horse freight   ...   .   1d.

POSTGATE OR POSKITE.

Before leaving the topography of old Hamilton, it may be mentioned in regard to this street that the proper name is Passgate. It is the remains of an old Roman road or gate from the Langloan that passed along the Castle Wynd, leading directly from the old boathouse through the Muir to Both-well Bridge. In times of danger, there was a sentry placed here, and a barricade erected, communicating with a fort at Castlehill, with another at the watch-tree, and finally with the Castle of Cadzow itself. This was, therefore, the Passgate, and was known as such long before ever a Post was known in Scotland.

THE UNREFORMED TOWN COUNCIL.

The affairs of the town were managed by a Coun-cil of twelve, including two bailies and a treasurer, who were elected annually in a sort of perpetual succession, the old appointing the new. Yearly a list of six was named by the expiring Council, and carried down to the Palace, out of which list the Duke named two bailies, generally the old ones. On a stated day these bailies appeared in the Court-house in the Tolbooth, and took the oaths, and then adjourned with the old Council to the Council-house, and there "choiced" a new Council, consisting commonly of their own noble selves without any change. In their nomination, the bailies are authorised to "administrat justice to the inhabitants of the burgh, and all others His Majesty's lieges, and to uplift and receive the fynes and emoluments pertaining to the said office, *and employ the same to their own uses.*"

CONVIVIALIA.

The magistrates exercised great diligence in exacting fines, but as there is no trace of any of them finding their way into the public purse, the inference is that they were applied to the purposes of refreshment during the many consultations held for the public welfare. If they were so applied it is clear they did not suffice for the purpose, for we have the tavern bills regularly and punctually settled every year along with the rest of the town's accounts. These were the times when vintners in name were vintners in reality, and when gentlemen and burgh magnates had the best of claret at the change house for some 18s or so a dozen. One William Simpson seems to have been the favourite vintner about the time of the Rebellion, and his wine account would come to from £20 to £30 yearly. But the Council did not confine their patronage to the regular dealers. They got their wine where they could get it best, and they seem at one time to have dealt regularly for the article with a medical gentleman, who, whatever he might know of the constitution of the body corporate, must have been qualified to judge of the appropriate stimulants for the bodies of the corporation. This gentleman was a James Naismith, chirurgeon, and his accounts are regularly settled year after year, with, in one instance, in the year 1731, "three shillings and fourpence money foresaid farder, as the price of two bottles whyte wine omitted out of the account, and which was drunk by the Baillies and Councill, with John Hamilton, one of his Graces's Commissioners." In the times somewhat later, we find the effect of the duties imposed on the juice of the grape indicated by the change of tipple to what is vaguely called "liquor," and by entries of expenses "for sugar and lemons." The harmonising effect of this generous system would seem to have been complete, as the authority we have already quoted leaves it on record that, in an examination of the Council minutes for a period of over 30 or 40 years, he could find no trace of any division in the Council.

THE COUNCIL AND PRINCE CHARLIE.

In 1745, Prince Charlie in his progress northwards stayed some days at Hamilton Palace, the noble owner of which was understood to be not unfavourable to his cause, and it is also well known that levies were made upon Glasgow for clothing and all sorts of supplies for the rebel army. The Council with great caution and prudence kept a "calm sough" as long as the enemy was at their door. No sooner had the last of the Highlanders crossed the Forth with the Duke of Cumberland's army in pursuit, than their loyalty was made to shine brilliantly forth, and, on the 4th of February 1746, "they appoint their treasurer to pay to Bailie Cunison four guineas for defraying his expenses in going in to Edinburgh to advise with the Lord-Justice Clerk as to the best way of behaving in the present conjuncture—how the town should behave most for the interest of the Government." This "four guineas" was all that the great Rebellion cost the town of Hamilton.

A TROUBLESOME JAILER.

John Hepburn was appointed town officer in 1731, and for many years held the four dignified appointments of town officer, jailer, keeper of the clock, and ringing of the bell, with all the fees and emoluments thereto belonging. John, however, was rather a convivial spirit, and did not always in his cups remember the propriety of demeanour due to the important offices he filled. Thus, on the 13th September, 1743, " Bailie Cunison represented to the Council that John Hepburn, jayler, hath several times, especially when drunk, been very abusive to the said Bailie, and that within these few days, being drunk, he gave the said Bailie a great deal of abusive language, and at the same time gave the Bailie the keys of the prison, which he had put into the hands of John Telfer, officer ; and the Council considering the same, they are of opinion that some fit person should be thought upon against next meeting of Council for supplying the office of jayler." John seems to have got a fright at his behaviour being thus seriously taken up, and to have made his peace with the Bailie and the Council, for there is no farther allusion to the affair, and, thirteen years afterwards, we find John Hepburn is still jailer, and town officer to boot, in all the glory of the coat and hat and ribbons, which awed the youth of ancient Hamilton into respect for the constituted authorities.

The other subordinate officers of the town at this time were—1, The town's officers—two in number— whose wages were raised in 1761 to 20s each per annum, besides the coats and hats and ribbons. 2, The town's drummer, who made all the more important announcements, and received 10s per annum for his services, besides a hat and coat, and 1s on the annual rouping days. 3, A town crier, first appointed in 1754, when his stations were fixed by the Council, and his remuneration settled at 1d stg. for each notice proclaimed. 4, A lamplighter, whose salary was £1 sterling, besides a "froak," which the town allowed him, no doubt, to save his clothes from the oil.

MAKING PROGRESS.

On the 29th of October, 1737, we find that "The Bailies and Council, in regard, it will be convenient, for the Burgh to have lamps through the town, appoint their treasurer to buy and put one on for a trial, and provide oil for the same, and to report the expense thereof betwixt and the next council day, and to put up the same at the corner of Bailie Muirhead's house. This lamp must, no doubt, have been considered a great success, and have been much admired by all the good burghers and their wives and bairns, for a dozen more were ordered, for the other parts of the town, before the winter was over. They were pretty dear, Bailie Muirhead's one costing £42 16s Scots, and the others £213 13s; but, no doubt, this was thought a cheap price for so great an improvement. Occasionally we find the Council making a grand exertion towards what we would call sanitary improvements; and, from what the minutes disclose, they seem to have had good reason. Thus, on 23d October, 1756, we find it recorded that "The Bailies and Council, having this day along with the sworn men of the burgh, visited the common loans, sheughs, and marches, in the Haugh, they, in the first place, find the Langloan is scarce passable by carts; therefore agree that the treasurer shall amend the same by gravelling the road up the Langloan from the Barns upwards, to where the road towards Ross crosses the Loan; they appoint intimation to be made by tuck of drum, on Monday next,

that the possessors of the lands in the Haugh do cast
sufficiently the sheughs in the Haugh against the
Monday following, certifying such as neglect that the
Bailies will cause do the work at the possessor's
charge, and the sworn men are to visit the same after
cast, to see that the same is sufficiently done, so as to
carry off the whole water. They find there should be
a covered syver for carrying the water across the road
at *Solomon's Vineyard.*" Then, after the various
details about the sheughs, the minute goes on—"And
appoint the midden, now lying in the street opposite
to Golder's and James Burnes's houses in the Townhead, to be removed, and the same to be filled up
with rubbish, and all other dunghills gathered on the
High Street, to be removed." The Council had a
proper estimate of the value of the commodity thus
stored in the public street, and it was only on a
written petition, and on his undertaking that he would
send all his fodder to be consumed in the town that
Mr John Campbell was allowed to remove some of it
for the cultivation of his land on the Muirbrow.

TREATMENT OF SOCIAL PROBLEMS.

There were paupers in those days, too ; and this is
how the increase of beggars was dealt with. On 2d
February, 1738, "The Magistrates and Town Councill, considering that of late the poor of this paroch
have considerably increased, and many of these
appear to be strangers from oyr. paroches, who
ought to be inhibited to the charity of this paroch,
for preventing and remeiding whereof, they do yrfor
appoint strict enquiry to be made with respect to the
poor who are strangers, and have not resided three
years in the paroch, that reports thereof be made to
the Councill to the end that such persons be turned
out of the paroch : And farder, prohibit and discharge

the heritors of this burgh, in time coming, to set
houses to strangers from other paroches, till such time
as they apply to one of the Magistrates of the Burgh
who may judge if the person who wants to take the
house have wherewith to maintain ymselves and
family, without being burdensome to the paroch;
and that under penalty of Twenty punds Scots,
to be exacted of the heritor who shall neglect to
make such previous application before settling; and
likeways appoint the officers of the burgh to seize and
apprehend all such strolling vagrant beggars as do not
reside within the paroch, and to the end the persons
who are proper objects of charity may be distinguished
from vagrants, they appoint publick intimation be
made through the Town of Hamilton by tuck of
drum, and placarding copies of this Act in the public
places, ordering all the persons who resolve to beg in
the paroch, that they present themselves and appear
before the Magistrates and Town Councill, in the
Tolbooth of Hamilton, the 13, 14, 15, and 16 days of
Feb. inst., at ten o'clock forenoon, that ye said
Baillies and Councill may enquire into these circumstances; and, upon finding them proper objects of
charity, give such persons badges to intitule them to
beg, which badges they appoint their treasurer to
have in readiness against that time, certifying all
such persons as shall be found begging in this Burgh
in time coming, not having such badges, that they
shall be punished as vagrants with the utmost
severity; and recommend to the Baillies to wait upon
the ministers and Kirk Session, and acquaint them
of, and lay before them this Act, and desire them to
make up lists of the poor of the country part of this
paroch, and give in the same to the said Bailies and
Town Councill, that they may likeways receive
badges." Accordingly, on the 22d of February, we

find it recorded that "The beggars being convened," the badges were given to the persons therein named, twelve in all, authorizing them to beg. The difficult problem of pauperism, however, was not to be so easily solved ; and, in a few years afterwards, we find again the same complaints of the increase of the poor ; and their character seems to have got worse, for the grievance is the "Allowing people to beg who can earn their bread without the charity of others, and allowing people to reside who are under the character of thieves and resetters of theft, and entertainers of vagrants and banished persons ;" and the Council remit to Bailie Semple, and others, to make up exact lists of all such persons, and report them on the next Wednesday.

MERCANTILE AFFAIRS.

Protection was the leading rule of trade. No hides were allowed to go out of the town until the town's tanner and shoemakers were first supplied. So also the price of bread was fixed from time to time, according to the price of wheat. Bakers were obliged to put their names, or initials, on their loaves —a practice still to some extent prevailing. Fines were imposed on butchers for cutting and hacking hides of the animals they killed, as well as for some operation called "tawing and blawing" in killing butcher meat. The same power and practice of regulation seems to have been applied to other trades. and where there was no law to warrant interference, the Bailies and Council passed resolutions, which they called Acts of Council, and which served the purpose nearly as well as Acts of Parliament. As one instance of this, amongst many, we may refer to a minute of date 14th October, 1736 :—"The Baillies and Councill agreed to the following rates to be paid to every horse-hyrer (in name of hyre) in manner

following, viz. :—That every man that is in use to let
horses for hyre be obliged to hyre his horses when
demanded, unless they can show that they are
oyrways necessary employed in journeying : That no
horse-hyrer pretend to demand more in name of hyre
than two shillings Scots for each mile single, and
three shillings Scots for each double horse, besides
half a-merk for every night the horse is kept, after
allowing the proper time for journeying in an ordinary
way, and that the owner of the horse who shall demand more, or exact any higher wages or hyre than
is a stipulat, shall, upon conviction yrof, be lyable in
a fyne of fourty shillings Scots money for each refusal
or contravention. They therefore appoint this Act to
be promulgat by tuck of drum, and placarded, that
none may pretend ignorance."

On market days and fair days, the various dealers
in the town, and the class called merchant travellers,
had stations assigned to them in the various streets,
and there they exposed their goods on stands for sale.
Thus, so late as 1766, we find it recorded that " The
Baillies and Councill agree to the following regulations
with regard to the merchants' stands at the fairs, viz.:—
The merchant travellers dealing in softwares shall
have their stands from the entry to the third shop
below the Tolbooth, and so eastward all upon the
north side of the street, leaving proper passage to
closes and shops—and the woollen cloth merchants
east of them. The merchants dealing in hardware
shall have their stand all upon south side of the High
Street, from the entry to John Mather's closs eastwards, and the nailers east of them. That the shoe
market shall be held on the south side of the School
Wynd, above the well. That the crockery merchants
shall stand to the west of the shoe market, south side
of School Wynd. That the dealers in sweetmeats

shall stand on the north side of the School Wynd,
from Alexander Wilson's house door westward."

Previously to 1732, the market for "horse and
nolt" was held on the high ground above the town,
now occupied by the Parish Church and churchyard,
and surrounding buildings; but in that year this
market had to be removed down to the streets of the
town on account of the building of the church, and
because, as the minute says—"the rest of the ground
will be taken up with houses which the town's
people will probably build for the conveniency of
being near the church." In 1736 there was a sheep
market instituted, to be held in May and June
yearly on the Muir, and so much of the Muir was
ordered to be cleared of whins as would be sufficient
for the sheep to stand and pasture upon it. This
market place was fenced in shortly afterwards "with
a pale dyke three feet and a half high, with stoups and
double rails"—the neighbouring tacksman, Thomas
Scoular, furnishing half of the nails necessary for the
dyke, according to express arrangement with Bailie
Porterfield.

The old burgess privileges were in full force. No
craftsman or merchant was allowed to carry on business on his own account within the town unless he
were a duly admitted burgess; and this privilege was
necessarily of much value, and considerable fees were
paid on admission—the amount of which, however,
was occasionally, in special circumstances, reduced,
and sometimes for the encouragement of trade, or to
confer special honour, a few favoured applicants were
admitted gratis. Thus, on 18th December, 1753,
" The Baillies and Councill appoint a gratis burgess-
ticket to be given to William Guthrie, skinner and
breachmaker, as being the first professor of that trade
in the Burgh." And ten years before, there is another

special case which, in the minutes of 12th March, 1743, is thus stated :—" It being represented by John Telfair, weaver in Hamilton ; Archd. Telfair, taylor, there ; and Thomas Craig, weaver, there, to the Baillies and Councill that Martinmas fair, 1741, the said Baillies being attacked by some of the Duke's servants, and they being very assistant to rescue them, the Baillies and Councill, for their reward, allow the Clerk to give them their burgess-ticket."

FIRES.

As the houses in the town had all, or nearly all, thatched roofs, there was, of course, great danger from fire, and the Bailies and Council occasionally enacted some laws to be observed for the public safety. One of these was passed on 21st January, 1740, and as it is very elaborate and somewhat peculiar in its provisions, we give its terms in full :—" The Baillies and Councill considering that the town of Hamilton consists gener- ally of thatched houses, and that frequent accident fires happen on account of the foulnes of the vents, there- fore, to prevent as much as possible such accidents, they authorise and appoint ———— to go through the town of Hamilton three times in the year—viz., Candlemass, Whitsunday, and Hallowmass—and to sweep and clean sufficiently the whole used vents in the town, at the following rates—viz., for each vent of the length of one storey, a penny ; and for those of a greater length, three halfpence; and to discharge all other ordi- nary sweepers to use that imployment, and appoint this Act to be intimat by tuck of drum throw the town of Hamilton, with a certification to such persons as shall refuse to allow their vents to be swept on pretence that they are not foull, if, upon a visitation, these vents are actually found to be foull, the person so refusing shall be lyable in a fyne of fourty shillings

Scots ; and the said authorised sweepers are by their acceptation of the office bound to make a careful visitation of all the vents, and to report to the Magistrates such persons as refuse to admit their vents, when foull, to be swept, under the penalty of being punished at discretion of the Baillies." Notwithstanding this rigid exactment, a very serious fire occurred in the town a few years later—a fire which history says raged for eight days, and burned down Barrie's Close and other adjacent parts of the town, and caused great misery to the inhabitants. It would seem that, on the usual principle of the precautions coming after the calamity, it led to the town getting its first fire-engine. In September 1748, "the Baillies and Councill considering the great use of a water engine for extinguishing fire, especially in this town where the houses are mostly thatched," agreed to buy one which was for sale in Edinburgh, and which cost £15 sterling, besides new leather pipes, which were got from Glasgow. A few months later, we find it noticed that collections had been set on foot in Edinburgh, and elsewhere for behoof of the sufferers by the late fire, and the Town Treasurer is authorised to receive the money, which was then to be issued forth at the direction of the Magistrates and Council.

A TIME OF SCARCITY.

It was in 1740, when "the Baillies and Councill, considering the present scarcity of meall, and the great hardships the inhabitants, and particularly the poor, now labour under, and understanding that John Mather is going to Perth Fair, where he may probably be informed where a quantity of meall may be bought at a reasonable rate, they therefore give commission to John Mather to contract for ane hundred bolls of sufficient meall upon the credit of

the community, providing the same can be bought so
as to be delivered at eight pounds Scots per boll at
Borrowstowness free of sea carriage."

HOUSE RENTS.

Shop and house rents were much less a century
ago than now. From the treasurer's abstract of
accounts we take the following sample :—Adam Roxburgh's shop for one year, from Whitsunday 1785 to
1786, £1 12s ; Andrew Hamilton's do., £1 1s ; Janet
Russell's house, £3 15s ; Wm. Buchanan's, £4 10s ;
Wm. Wilson's shop 16s 8d ; Janet Hyslop's shop, £1
1s. These figures may well excite envy amongst a
community overridden with exorbitant rents, and
striving hard to release themselves from the burden.

A PIOUS BELLMAN.

If, at one time, Hamilton had her inebriate John
Hepburn, she was at another time famed for a bell-
man or church-officer of another sort. He was a rigid
observer of family worship. In his devotions, however, he had an eye to this world as well as the next.
One morning his wife had neglected to bar the door,
and when Sandy had got about half-way through his
prayer, a person entered to purchase a pennyworth of
something from the mistress, who kept a small shop.
The ounce weight had gone amissing, and could not
be found. The modern Pharisee, with the view of
helping his better half out of her difficulty, paused,
and by way of parenthesis said, in a less whining tone
of voice, "As for the ounce weight, Jenny, ye shall
find it amongst the wee bits o' ben leather on the
window bottom ; may the Lord preserve us frae
formality and carnality !" and then he resumed his
long prayer.

CHARITY SCHOOLS A CENTURY AGO.

So far back as 1789, a charity school was erected in Hamilton, of which Mr James Bruce was school-master. This school was kept up for many years. Annual premiums were distributed, and, as they are rather novel, we give a few specimens. For the boys —To the best reader in the Bible, a scarlet bonnet with a silver button; for the best reader in the New Testament, a scarlet bonnet; for the best reader in the A B C, 2d. For the girls—To the best reader in the Bible, a mutch of Holland, with a head suit of ribbons; to the best reader in the New Testament, a necklace; to the best reader in Proverbs, a new Testament; to the best reader in the Question Book, a napkin; to the best reader in the A B C, 2d. These children met every Sabbath day between sermons, when the bell rung, and repeated their questions before the congregation. About the same period, another school was instituted by the Duchess of Hamilton for little maiden orphans, where they were taught to spin and work lace. The lace, under the name of Hamilton lace, rose into high repute, so much so that the trustees for encouraging fisheries and manufactures in Scotland, destined £75 for encourage-ment to young beginners—every young scholar to have £1 at the end of the first year of their apprenticeship, and £15 to be divided into prizes amongst them. A large house and garden, rent free, newly mounted—now the old manse of Hamil-ton—was set aside for the purpose of a school-house. A number of subscribers also contributed to the "Orphan Hospital." About £3 yearly was con-sidered a sufficient sum to maintain each orphan in meat, clothing, &c. After much labour on the part of its promoters, the scheme was laid aside.

The population of the parish, which in 1755 was 3815, had increased in 1841 to 10,861, being at the rate of nearly 82 per annum. The means of communication with the outer world had more than kept pace. "Davie Hamilton's Caravan"—a lumbering, covered one-horse cart—gave way to the stage-coach, which in turn was replaced by the iron horse. Apropos of the " Caravan," it started from Hamilton at 6 A.M., and reached an old inn in the Gallowgate, near Charlotte Street, at 11. Davie drove himself, and never allowed his Rozinante to trot except for a short distance down hill. The return journey was made at 4 P.M., and the party reached Hamilton about 8. In winter, the company were sometimes favoured with a "bawbee" candle. As time went on, the town began to spread its wings to the south and west. The great highway between Glasgow and London, ran through the burgh, and for the purpose of avoiding the brae in Muir Street and cutting off the awkward elbow at the Cross, about the year 1847, the road was diverted into the present line of Cadzow Street. The new road is upwards of 700 yards in length, and it is carried over the Cadzow burn above the public green by a bridge of three arches, each 60 feet span, which Mr Patrick, writing at the time, not inaccurately described as stupendous, the top of the parapet wall being 60 feet above the bed of the burn. The town began to lose much of its pleasant rural appearance. No longer was the quiet of Muir Street to be disturbed by the din of the stage-coach in its daily passage through the burgh, and Castle Street, as the leading thoroughfare, was doomed. Along the new line of route, handsome banks and shops sprung into existence, and Cadzow Street became the centre of trade

and business. The opening of the Caledonian Central
Railway Station threatens to raise in Quarry Street
a formidable rival, and already first-class shops are
occupied by energetic, pushing tradesmen—some of
them from Cadzow Street and Townhead Street; and
after the improvements which are in contemplation
have been carried out, there are not wanting signs
that ere long this neighbourhood will become the
centre of the burgh. Forty years ago there were no
buildings on the west side of Cadzow Street, except a
few one-storey thatched houses near the foot of Campbell Street. Auchingramont Road, Park Road, and
Clydesdale Street were not in existence, while nearly
all the properties along the line of Union Street and
west-end of the town have been subsequently built.
Hand-loom weaving was the staple trade of the town,
and the nearest coal-pit was several miles away. Now
all is changed, the weavers with the appliances of their
craft are almost totally extinct, and there are no less
than 12 pits almost within the bounds of the burgh,
and fully as many more within a mile of it. Glasgow
merchants were attracted by the woodlands and the
pure air, and made their homes in the suburb of vil-
las in the west-end. The geological situation of the
coal measures—and probably also Hamilton Palace—
were a guarantee that the neighbourhood would not
soon share the fate of so many pleasant districts in the
west. Here was still an oasis where the eye could
wander over undulating fields and tree-clad heights
yet untouched by the indomitable mercantile spirit
which has converted the Clyde valley into a teeming
hive of industry. The abnormal prices and demand
for coal and iron during 1872-73-74 changed all this,
and now the amenity of the district has to be sacrificed
for the good of the country at large. Railways have
cut it up in all directions; its romantic rocks serve but

for piers to the unromantic girder bridge ; and over the trees rises the coalpit head-gear, with its attendant chimney stalk, darkening the air with smoke and smudge.

THE COAL INDUSTRY.

In the new statistical account of the parish of Hamilton, written in 1835 by the Rev. Wm. Patrick, the coal field of the district is thus described :—" Coal is chiefly wrought at Quarter, about three miles south of the town of Hamilton. The same bed also extends a great way northwards in the direction of Glasgow, but owing to a slip in the coal metals between the farms of Simpsonland and Carscallan, a little to the north of Quarter, the coal is sunk nearly 100 fathoms below its usual level ; an accident which puts it almost beyond the reach of the inhabitants of Hamilton, Blantyre, and part of Bothwell : the strata not rising up again till near Cambuslang. The existence of this remarkable fracture is indicated by the coal metals on the banks of the Avon, and the other burns below where the break occurs, all dipping to the southwest ; whereas above that particular spot they, and indeed the whole strata of the district, with this single exception, dip to the north-east. The coal strata here resemble those throughout the county. At Quarter, the first bed worth working is the ten feet or woman's coal, so called because it was once wrought by females. This is a soft coal, which burns rapidly ; and although called the ten feet coal, is in reality from 7 to 14 feet in thickness. Fifteen fathoms lower down, the ell coal occurs, so called because it was first found of that thickness ; but it is frequently from 4 to 6 feet thick. In the fire it cakes, or runs into a mass, and is much esteemed by blacksmiths. Ten or fifteen fathoms below the former is the seam called the main coal. This, at Quarter, is 5 feet 6 inches thick, and consists of four distinct varieties of coal—1st, The ground coal, undermost, 20 inches thick, gummy and sooty : 2d, immediately above it the yolk, or jet coal, 6 inches thick, of a fine clear vitreous texture, like cannel coal, affording abundance of light ; 3d, parrot coal, 10 inches ; 4th, splint coal, about 30 inches. This is the coal now wrought, both by shanks and ingoing pits. The shanks at Quarter are about 30 fathoms. The mouths of the ingoing pits are on the banks of the Avon, about two miles above Hamilton. These pits communicate with each other. The coal is brought from Quarter by a railway along the banks of the Avon, and is laid down at Avon bridge, half-a-mile from Hamilton, at 3s 9d a ton. Upwards of 10,000 tons are here sold annually. About half that quantity is disposed of at Quarter to people in the upper side of the parish, and the adjacent parishes of Glassford, Avondale, and Kilbride."

EARLY MINING OPERATIONS.

Coal has been wrought at Quarter from an early period for the use of the surrounding district. As an evidence of the antiquity of the workings, it may be stated that, about forty or fifty years ago, some workmen penetrated into an old mine which entered from the banks of the Avon, and on exploring it they discovered a pick and shovel of a very primitive con-struction, being made of wood, and shod or pointed with iron. The mine was in good order, and the mode of working it had been very secure. The coal was hewn out in the form of an arch, having " a heat coomceiled roof," as one of the exploring party described it to Mr Andrew Hamilton. It has been supposed that these old workings date as far back as the time when Cadzow Castle was inhabited--some 300 years ago. As the uppermost seam, called the soft coal, crops out here, it appears to have been wrought first by running a mine into the face of a brae, which was called " an ingaun ee." By cutting a *gatten* or gutter in the pavement of this mine it formed a drain to carry off the water from " the faces " or " rooms," as the working places were named. This mine was called a " level," and the coal thus drained was said to be " level free," which was considered a great advantage by miners in the olden time, when there was no pumping apparatus. The coal was taken to the mouth of the mine in corfs or hutches, which were drawn along the pavement. As the road soon became rough and the draught heavy after the mine was driven in a certain distance, it was deemed more expedient and profitable to sink a pit to the coal, and thus save the heavy labour of drawing. These pits being ebb (from 8 to 10 fathoms) the coals in the hutches were raised to the surface by a hand windlass, and emptied in cartloads on the *hill*, as they were sold by measure before the introduction of the weighing machine. When it became necessary to sink a deeper shaft the gin superseded the windlass, and after the introduction of steam the gin gave place to the winding engine.

RECENT OPERATIONS AT QUARTER.

The Quarter collieries were till within the last thirty years held in the possession of the proprietor, the Duke of Hamilton, and were under the charge of a " grieve," or manager, who sold the coals, paid the workmen, and transacted all the business of the works, for which he was accountable to the Chamberlain at Hamilton Palace. One pit at Quarter was sufficient to supply the country sale up to the year

1854, when the mineral field was leased by the Messrs Dunlop of Clyde Ironworks, after which its resources were fully developed. Boring operations were then commenced, and a bed of excellent black-band ironstone discovered about 15 fathoms below the main coal. The seams called the slatey and clay band were also found at Darngaber and Boghead. Pits were sunk to them, a large quantity put out and calcined, and more pits were sunk to the coal. In 1856 two furnaces were built for the manufacture of pig iron, and put in blast in March 1857. A third was built in 1867, a fourth in 1869, and a fifth in 1875. Owing to the depression of trade, only three are in blast at present. The average production of pig-iron from each furnace is about $8\frac{1}{2}$ thousand tons a year. The ironstone at Quarter has been wrought out, but the company have pits at Boghead, Blantyre, and Drummine, from which large supplies of ore are brought to the furnaces. The limestone required is also brought from Blantyre and Lesmahagow.

Of five coal pits four are in operation just now, the output from which may be stated at 120,000 tons yearly. Besides supplying the furnaces, a large quantity of coal is sent to the market. After the opening of the Hamilton and Strathaven Railway, in 1862, a branch line was made to the works, which greatly facilitated the mineral traffic. As it requires about 150 men to supply material for each furnace, upwards of 500 hands of all kinds are employed in connection with the works.

OVERCOMING THE "ACCIDENT."

The "accident" mentioned by Mr Patrick, by which the coal was sunk almost beyond the reach of the inhabitants of Hamilton, Blantyre, and Bothwell, has been successfully overcome by the aid of capital, improved machinery, and modern appliances for the working of mines. In 1856, twenty years after Mr Patrick wrote, the mineral under Dykehead and High Merryton, extending to 597 acres, was leased by his Grace the Duke of Hamilton to the Summerlee Iron Company, by whom the field is still wrought. A still more conspicuous proof that the "accident" had been overcome, was the leasing in 1858-59 of the mineral in connection with the estate of Greenfield, to the west of the town, by Mr Lewis Potter to Mr James Nisbet. The need of mechanical appliances and engineering skill of the first order was very emphatically demonstrated in the Greenfield case. The quantity of water and other physical difficulties that were encountered and had to be overcome in the act of reaching the coal exhausted' Mr Nisbet's considerable means. After his withdrawal from the concern, operations were continued by the Hamilton Coal Company, by whom the colliery is worked at the present time. The Ferniegair Colliery, on the Larkhall Road, extending to 230 acres, was successfully worked on lease from his Grace the Duke of Hamilton by Mr James Nisbet from 1859 to 1861 ; by Messrs James Nisbet & Co. till 1866 ; and since that date by Mr A. Russell, who a year or two ago acquired the additional right to work the mineral lying underneath Chatelherault Park. In the same locality, the Merryton Colliery was opened up by the Duke, who in 1860 granted a lease of the same to Messrs Cochrane & Brand. The colliery in their hands has been remarkably successful. Three years ago it was closed for six months—fire, believed to be the result of spontaneous combustion, having broken out in the workings. The firm acquired an additional field under the High Parks in 1865. In 1862, the Allanton field, still in the same neighbourhood, extending to 340 acres, was leased by his Grace to Messrs Austine & Co., who also in 1865 had an additional field in the High Parks added to their workings. This fruitful part of the Clyde basin was not yet exhausted, and in 1864 the Duke leased the Merryton Home Farm field, of 160 acres, to Messrs Hamilton, M'Culloch & Co. The unparalleled inundation, which in a few hours, on a dark January morning of 1877, ruined the working of the colliery, and deprived four men of life, is elsewhere noticed. With unflagging zeal and energy, the acting partner of the firm, Mr Kirkwood, has had the chasm, which was created by the action of the water, pumped dry, and the workings are being redd with good prospects of operations at the colliery being again resumed. In 1865, Messrs John Watson & Son leased Bog and Highlees, about 320 acres, and transferred the colliery in 1871 to Messrs Hamilton & M'Culloch. A year later, in 1866, a lease of the South Haugh field or Haughhead, about 100 acres, was taken up by Messrs Merry & Cuninghame, and in 1877 was transferred to the present lessee, Mr John M'Donald.

THE COAL IN THE TOWN'S LANDS.

That one day coal would be found in the town's lands was the fond belief of more than one generation of Hamiltonians, and the prophecy was indulged that the town would yet become a Coatbridge. At last, in 1838, a citizen of great public spirit, Mr Daniel M'Arthur, lace manufacturer, made application to the Town Council for a lease of the mineral. His application, which came before the Council on 13th January, 1838, was in the following terms :—" I hereby make offer to the Magistrates and Town Council of Hamilton for a twelve years' lease of the coal within the burgh

lands of Hamilton, and to pay therefor of fixed yearly
rent the sum of £100 stg., or in the option of the
proprietors, one-ninth of the coal sold or removed
from the pit-mouth or coal hill of lordship, payable
said rents half-yearly at Martinmas and Whitsunday,
and in respect that it has yet to be ascertained
whether there are coals in said lands, and whether
they may be worth working, it is understood that I
am to have full power and liberty to bore, search for,
use means for ascertaining what metals are in the
lands, and that only at my own expense ; and that
the said rent or lordship shall not commence until
the workings are begun and a regular output of coals
given.   Further, that I shall not be bound to continue
the lease should the coal or mineral turn out imprac-
ticable and unprofitable, and it is also understood that
should the experiment prove successful that I shall
enter into a regular lease containing all the usual
clauses contained in those most approved of in the
county consistent with this offer, and that I shall
have right to use the roads connected with the town's
lands, as well as to drive levels, shank pits, and make
railroads or other roads necessary for said work, and
erect engines for carrying on the same.   I shall be
bound in addition to said rent to pay all surface
damages that I may occasion, the same to be ascertained by men to be mutually chosen; and it is understood that any engines, implements, or effects, which
I may lay down or erect shall belong to me, and be
at my disposal at the termination of the lease, the
proprietors having the first offer thereof on a fair
valuation."   This offer being taken into consideration,
the Council, after due deliberation, " and considering
that coal may not be found, and if found that it is
likely to be attended with heavy expense in the
working thereof," unanimously accepted of the same,

accompanying their acceptance with five conditions, the principal of which was that the trial for coal was to be made and completed by Mr M'Arthur within six months. The likelihood of coal being found seems to have strongly impressed itself on the minds of the members of Council, as at this same meeting they passed a resolution directing the clerk in all future feu contracts to be granted by the Magistrates and Council to insert a clause reserving the metals and minerals to the town. Hitherto there had been no such reservation, and at the present time a committee of Town Council is engaged negotiating with those feuars who are lucky enough to hold their charters from a date prior to the passing of this resolution for the purchase of their rights in the coal.

Mr M'Arthur appears to have vigorously prosecuted the necessary boring operations during the six months allowed him, though not successfully. On 19th August a special meeting of Town Council was held, to consider a motion relative to the operations. On behalf of Mr M'Arthur, Mr Gowans informed the meeting that he had bored to a depth of 75 fathoms, whereby he had expended about £200, that both the appearance of the metals and strata throughout indicated the prospect of there being coal in the lands; but the six months allowed him for the trial having expired, he was not inclined at his own expense to proceed further at present. He, however, recommended the town to carry the bore down other ten fathoms, giving it as his opinion that before that depth was reached the coal would be found, if it was in the lands capable of being wrought to any advantage; and he accompanied his recommendation with an intimation of his willingness to present to the town gratis, if they continued the bore for the ten fathoms, his windlass, triangle, lever, ropes, and other implements used by him in making the trial. The Council did not deem it advisable to follow out the suggestion made to them. They passed a resolution placing it on record that they were sensible of the exertions and perseverance of Mr M'Arthur in proceeding so far, and incurring so much expense in the trial, and unanimously voted him their thanks on that account. The resolution not to continue the trial, it should be explained, was only carried by a majority of three votes, and Mr M'Arthur's bore was ordered to be plugged up and secured "so as at any after period the town might have recourse to it in facilitating the trial for coal or other minerals" in their lands.

After this, all idea of developing the mineral resources of the town, if not abandoned, was allowed to go to sleep. For twenty years the Council records make no mention of the subject. The long silence was at last broken by the receipt of a letter, which was considered at the monthly meeting on 6th June, 1859, in these terms:—

"Drumpark, Coatbridge, 2d June, 1859.—Dear Sir,—I have been requested by a party to inquire if the coal in the town's lands of Hamilton are to be let, and should that be the case to inform me as to the mode or principle upon which an offer might be framed. Your early answer will oblige, &c.,
(Signed)   "WM. M'CREATH."

The Council appointed a committee to report how far it would be expedient to entertain any proposal for letting the mineral. Next month the committee reported in favour of letting the mineral, the town to be at no expense in boring or otherwise testing the coal field, or in the putting down of shafts or pits. The Council were not satisfied with the information laid before them, and the committee were re-appointed with instructions to report further details, and employ an engineer if they saw fit. The committee consulted Mr William M'Creath, M.E., who stated that the surface under which the town had it in their power to work the minerals, including roads, railway, &c., was about 85 acres Imperial, under all of which the several seams of coal contained in the Clydesdale basin might be confidently expected, and of quality and thickness similar to what was found both on the east and the west of the burgh. The position of the blackband ironstone was also throughout the whole field, but its lay was more capricious than that of the coals, and its being found in the lands was more uncertain. The Town Council followed up this procedure by advertising the let of the minerals. At their meeting on 5th December an offer was produced from Mr James Nisbet, Provost of the burgh, and at the time engaged in his Greenfield undertaking. The offer does not appear to have come up to the Council's expectations, and a committee appointed to consider and report upon it having recommended to the meeting on 5th March, 1860, that the offer be not entertained, all further reference to the subject vanishes once more from the records, and does not again appear for more than ten years afterwards.

For a third, and, as it proved, last time, the question was brought before the Council on 7th March, 1872. It was seriously taken up, and that Mr James Mackie, who has since been appointed burgh chamberlain, had the matter in charge, was a guarantee that nothing would be left undone to successfully carry it out. The form of the Council's action was to appoint Bailie Cassels and Mr Mackie, the latter convener, a committee to consider if, and in what way, the minerals could be made available. The negotiations were tedious and protracted, and extended over a period of two years; but the untiring perseverance of the committee eventually surmounted every obstacle. On 19th February, 1874, an offer by Dr Thomson, Jerviston House, Motherwell, and Mr R. L. Alston, Newfield House, Hamilton, " to take on lease the whole coal down to and including the splint seam in the town's lands of Hamilton, to be worked along with the coal in the lands of Wellhall, which we have purchased, and that in the lands of Nether Auchingramont, which has been leased by us," was accepted. The arrangement included a fixed rent of £350 per annum, commencing to run at Whitsunday, 1878, to be increased by £50 annually until it reached £500, at which it was to remain during the remainder of the lease, or, in the option of the proprietors, a lordship of 10d for each 22½ cwt. of coal and dross unscreened that was put out. The lease was to be for 31 years from Whitsunday, 1873, with breaks in the tenants' option at the end of the sixth and every third year thereafter. The arrangement was an important and favourable one for the burgh, and the committee were awarded a vote of thanks for carrying it out.

In addition to Wellhall and Nether Auchingramont, the lessees acquired the right to work the coal under Backmuir and Barmichael Plantations, belonging to the Duke of Hamilton, and extending to 300 acres. The collieries more than two years ago were taken up by the Clyde Coal Company (Limited) who have also pits in course of being sunk at Spittalhill, Cambuslang. Those at Hamilton admit of an output of 1200 tons a day restricted, on account of dull trade, to 700 tons. Above ground the works have been planned on an extensive scale. The permanent buildings, which have all been constructed of red brick with white facings, include the necessary engine-houses for the

winding gear and pumps; engineers', joiners', and
blacksmiths' shops, a pay office, with enclosed yard,
round which are sheds to protect the men in wet
weather, while waiting for their turn at the window,
and the general offices of the company. The
machinery which has been put up is of a very powerful
description, commensurate with the heavy work it
has to perform in raising coal hutches from such
a depth. Each of the winding engines has a 24-inch
cylinder with a 5-feet stroke, all the boilers being of
the tubular type, with the latest improvements for
securing economy of fuel. The shafts, it may be said,
are 24 feet by 7 feet in section, and are each divided
into three parts by strong wooden partitions techni-
cally known as brattices; the pumping gear working
in one division and the "cages" in the others. The
sides of the shafts are strongly lined with wood. As
it is estimated that the hutches pass up and down at
a speed of 20 miles an hour, it was necessary that the
framework over the pit mouth should be of a most
substantial character. This has not been lost sight of,
and all the head-gear, here as elsewhere, has a very
durable appearance. To ventilate the pits, a fan of
large dimensions, driven by steam, is employed, and
is powerful enough to keep air circulating freely in
the three pits. A private line connects the colliery
with the Hamilton branch of the Caledonian Railway,
and every convenience in the shape of stages and
separating screens for loading the waggons has been
provided.

In connection with their pits at Hamilton, nearly
300 houses for the accommodation of workmen have
been built by the Company in a field at Burnbank,
half a mile west from the colliery. The houses, which
are of brick, with stone facings, are all two storeys in
height, divided into quarter flats, each containing a

room and kitchen, having a little strip of garden ground
attached.

CADZOW AND OTHER COLLIERIES.

Both for the scale upon which they are laid out,
and the large capital embarked in the enterprise, the
Cadzow Company's collieries at Low-waters may be
selected for special notice. The coalfield, which
covers an area of upwards of 500 acres, has been
leased by the company from his Grace the Duke of
Hamilton. It extends from the Strathaven road to
the Avon, being situated almost wholly within the
High Parks of Hamilton, and it contains all the usual
seams of coal of the district. By bores put down it
was known that the first seam, the celebrated household ell coal of the district, would be found at a depth
of 244 yards below the surface. For the winning of
the coal, three pits were sunk. These consisted of No. 1,
the pumping pit, 24 ft. 6 in. × 7 ft. : No. 2, 21 ft. 6
in. × 6 ft. ; and No. 3, a round pit, built from top to
bottom, 13 ft. 6 in. within the brick work. Commenced in 1872, the work of sinking proved one of
unprecedented difficulty. Water was encountered at
a depth of only twelve feet from the surface, and two
sets of pumps had to be put in, both in No. 1 and
No. 2 pits. The obstacle assumed serious proportions
when the red rock was reached, and 6000 tons of
water fell to be removed from the shaft every twenty-
four hours. To accomplish this, the company erected a
Cornish engine of great size and power, having an
85-in. cylinder with a 10-ft. stroke, and being one of the
largest in Scotland. The pumps of the engine are 26
inches in diameter, the pump rods 18 inches square,
strapped with iron $7\frac{1}{2}$ inches broad and $1\frac{1}{2}$ inches
thick. Before the indomitable perseverance and
energy of the managing partner of the company, Col.
Austine, Oak Lodge, Hamilton, every obstacle had

eventually to give way, and the mineral was struck
in No. 2 Pit on the 3d of February, 1876 ; in No. 3
Pit a few weeks afterwards, and in No. 1 still later.
In No. 2 Pit the ell coal was struck at 123 fathoms.
The other two shafts are carried down to the splint
seam, which was tapped at a depth of 148 fathoms or
888 feet. One of the shafts—the upcast—is constructed in a circular form, 13 ft. 6 in. in diameter,
and is lined with brick instead of wood from top to
bottom. The pit fittings are of an advanced description. Three permanent coupled winding engines set
on concrete seats have been erected, their cylinders
being 24 in., with 5-ft. stroke, and for the purposes of
ventilation a Guibal fan, by Haggie & Co., New-
castle, 40 feet in diameter and 12 feet broad, has
been set up, and the fan house is connected to the
upcast shaft by a tunnel 12 feet in diameter. The
fan is driven by a 36-inch cylinder engine, stroke 3
feet ; and, in case of repairs being needed, there is a
reserve engine of the same size and power which can
be connected in a few minutes. A little village has
sprung up at the collieries, which are connected with
the Caledonian line at Hamilton by a branch line one
and a half miles long. The estimated output from all
the pits when in full operation is 1500 tons per day—
in the present state of trade it is, of course, greatly less.

But a short distance from Cadzow, are the
Eddlewood Coal Company's pits, and coming down
the hill, within a few hundred yards of each other
and half encircling the town, there are the collieries
of Barncluith and Silvertonhill (A. Russell), Bent
(Bent Colliery Company), Allanshaw (Allanshaw Coal
Company), and Earnock (John Watson), Taking up
the circle Blantyre wise, and not mentioning Messrs
Dunlop's ironstone pits, there fall to be enumerated
the new collieries, all recently opened up, of Dyke-

head (Dunn & Ure), Blantyre (W. Dixon, Limited), Auchinraith (Merry & Cuninghame); and towards Bothwell, the collieries of Craighead and Bothwell Park—collieries just opened up, or in course of being opened up by Messrs Wm. Baird & Co. The list might be greatly extended by continuing it to Cambuslang, where on the lands of that name the Flemington Company have sunk the deepest pit in Scotland—the depth to the splint coal being 212 fathoms, or a quarter of a mile.

In estimating the effect of so many new collieries on the market, one or two important considerations must be kept in view. In the first place, all the fixed rents are large ; and next, the amount of capital required to "win" the coal from such depths is very heavy. It is, therefore, only by sending a large supply of coal into the market that these expensive undertakings can be made to pay ; and, having that in view, it is estimated that, when all the pits have been got into full working order, and making allowance for bad times and the other contingencies of mining, the output from the Hamilton and Bothwell district cannot be less than 2,000,000 tons per annum. In round numbers, this field has an area of 8000 acres, and as it is computed to contain 300,000,000 tons of coal it will doubtless be one of the principal coal-producing districts in Scotland for two or three generations to come. The capital embarked in the undertaking is estimated at over one million sterling. The following figures, taken from the Valuation Roll for the current year, will throw further light on the value of the coal industry of the district :—

Burgh and Parish of Hamilton, ...	£55,465
Parish of Blantyre, ...	9,301
Parish of Bothwell, ...	19,271
Total, ...	£84,037

MEMORABLE ACCIDENTS.

An explosion of fire-damp took place on 16th March, 1841, at a pit at Avon Bank, resulting in the death of 13 men. The pit was commenced about 1825 by his Grace the Duke of Hamilton. From 150 to 200 hands were employed, the mode of working being by ingoing "eyes." Such terrible calamities were rare in those days, and the effect of the news on the town was paralysing. As to the circumstances under which the explosion occurred, one man had been burned the day previous. This did not arouse alarm, and the colliers resumed work on the morning of the accident as usual. They were not, however, long in the mine when the explosion took place, killing seven men. An hour after the explosion, an exploring party of nine, including Mr Ord Adams, the manager, entered the workings, and four of their number died from the effects of after-damp. We believe that Mr Adams, and a miner named Michael Forrest, Quarter, are the only survivors of those who formed the exploring party. A widow of one of the victims (Mrs Duffy, Quarter), still lives, and is a pensioner on the Duke's bounty. On Wednesday, 7th August, 1861, the community had again emphatically brought home to them the dangers of the mine by a disastrous and fatal fire, which broke out about 1 P.M. at Dykehead Colliery, Larkhall, in the occupation of the Summerlee Iron Company. The fire, beginning in the air shaft, destroyed the pit-head framework and burned the wooden casing of the shaft. The law had not yet made the double shaft imperative, and all communication with the men in the workings, 50 in number, was cut off. As invariably happens, there were not wanting many willing to risk their lives to rescue those imprisoned below ground, and by the persevering efforts of the managers, workmen, and others, the last of them had been brought to the surface by one o'clock next morning. It was found that 12 had been suffocated by the foul air, and one died afterwards, making the record of victims 13. The year 1877 will ever possess a black eminence in the mining annals of the district. On the morning of the 23d of January a disastrous inundation occurred at Home Farm Colliery. Between 50 and 60 miners had been lowered to the pit bottom, when the water burst into the ell workings, filling them in the course of a few hours with silt and water. The men, with the exception of four were got out in safety. In October of this year the incidents of the catastrophe were recalled by workmen engaged in excavations, with the view to resuming working at the Colliery, finding the remains of the four victims lying thickly imbedded in the sand. The most disastrous of mining accidents, not merely in this district, but in Scotland, took place at Nos. 2 and 3 Pits, High Blantyre Collieries, on the 22d of October, 1877. There had not been lacking warnings of the fiery character of the splint seam of the district, two explosions on a considerable scale having within the previous nine months occurred no farther away than Cadzow, which, while happily unattended with loss of life, resulted in the Colliery on each occasion being for some time closed. Nor had coalmasters failed to profit by these warnings, by attention to ventilation, the use of the most approved safety lamps, &c. Despite of every precaution, the explosion occurred, depriving 212 men and boys of life. Of 233 who were at work at the time but 27 escaped, 4 others who were brought up alive having soon afterwards died. The calamity awakened national sympathy, and that the widows and children of the lost might be provided for, nearly £50,000 was subscribed. In the spring of this year an accident from over-winding occurred at No. 3 Pit, Blantyre Collieries, by which six men were killed.

QUARTER.

(By Mr Andrew Hamilton.)

THE lands of Quarter form a portion of the ducal estate of Hamilton, and are situated on the south side of the wall which surrounds the High Parks of Hamilton. They stretch along the banks of the Avon from that wall to the march of Fairholm on the east, marching with Thinacres and Wellbog on the south and Darngaber and Carscallan on the west, and extend to upwards of 400 acres imperial.

In a rent roll of the Hamilton estates for 1637, in the time of James 3d Marquis of Hamilton, they are designed "The fiftie pund lands of Quarter," and were then divided into 8 " Rooms " or holdings, and possessed by the following tenants :—George Golder, younger; John Thomson, George Golder, elder; William Golder, John Wilson, Andrew Haddow, John Stobo, and John Alstoun."

In the year 1745, a meeting of the heritors and tenants of the parish was convened at Hamilton, to consider a demand made on them for supplies of forage and corn for the use of Prince Charles—Edward's cavalry then occupying Glasgow. The following names from Quarter appear in the list of heritors and tenants then convened :—" Wm. Wilson, in Quarter ; Andrew Haddow, there ; James Wilson, there ; John Hamilton, in Laigh Quarter." It thus appears that the 8 holdings of 1637 had been converted into 4 by the year 1745. The lands are now divided into three farms—named South Quarter, North Quarter, and Knowetop—tenanted respectively by Abram Torrance, Andrew Hamilton, and John Fleming. Part of the old farm of Laigh Quarter is let for grazing.

Part of the old houses of High and Low Quarter are remnants of the farm steadings, or "touns," occupied by the land tenants, when it was more sub-divided than at present. Their architecture is of a very rough order, and that part of them named "The Divoty" indicates the material of which it was origin-ally constructed. They were about twenty in num-ber. After the opening of the mines in Avon braes, about sixty years ago, some 15 or 20 additional houses were built at Low Quarter for the accommoda-tion of the workmen employed there.

As coals in the olden time were only required for household purposes, the demand in summer was limited, and in that season the colliers at Quarter were not regularly employed, so that they had to turn their attention to "country wark," such as work-ing in stone quarries and lime works, and with the farmers at hay-time and harvest. Being economical and thrifty, they were mostly all "bein" and well-to-do. A number of them kept cows for the use of their families, and all of them a pig—a practice which still prevails among the descendants of "the old residenters."

When the works were extended by the Messrs Dunlop, a large number of houses were built in the neighbourhood of the furnaces; so that there are now more than 200 houses in connection with the works, besides a great number rented by the work-men at Darngaber, Wellbog, Limekilnburn, and other places.

Before the extension of the works, the population of the old village of High and Low Quarter was about 200. In 1861 it stood thus—

Quarter Ironworks,	...	...	...	461
High Quarter,	...	...	...	60
Low Quarter,	...	...	...	140
	Total,		...	661

In 1871—

Quarter Ironworks,	...	...	...	544
High Quarter,	...	...	...	76
Low Quarter,	...	...	...	178
	Total,		...	798

The following census was taken in 1877 by Mr Allan, the police constable stationed at Quarter, of the district under his charge, lying on the south and west sides of the parish of Hamilton. With the exception of the farmers and cottars and the inhabitants of Earnockmuir Rows, the most of the householders of the other places specified are employed about the works. 1877—

Quarter Ironworks,	...	...	...	695
High Quarter,	...	...	...	60
Low Quarter,	...	...	...	149
Carscallan Rows,	...	...	...	120
Boghead Rows,	...	...	...	80
Plotcock,	...	...	...	38
Darngaber,	...	...	...	40
Wellbog,	...	...	...	23
Limekilnburn,	...	...	...	99
Earnockmuir Rows,	...	...	...	62
Farmers and Cottars,	...	...	...	418
	Total,		...	1784

On the farm of Darngaber the field is still pointed out where Gordon of Earlston was killed by a party of English dragoons, after the defeat of the Covenan-

ters at Bothwell Bridge. It is called Allows Hill—
perhaps a corruption of Earlston's Hill; and I
remember a stunted thorn tree, "worn by the knaw-
ing tooth of Time," which the old people in the
district held in reverence, and said marked the spot
where the martyr fell. It is stated by tradition
that, after putting him to death in the most barbar-
ous manner, they seized his horse, stripped him of
his accoutrements, including a pair of silver spurs,
and rode back to Carscallan—a neighbouring farm
town—where the English officer demanded refresh-
ments for his men, ostentatiously displaying his spoil
with many imprecations, which roused the feelings of
the goodwife of the house, who indignantly exclaimed
—"It becomes a better man than you, sir, to wear
these." After rifling the house of provisions, they
rode off towards Hamilton, giving vent to their rage
against the Covenanters by oaths and ribaldry.
Gordon was buried by his friends secretly in the
churchyard of Glassford, about two miles southwards
from the place where he fell, where a monument has
been erected to his memory by one of his descendants, which tells of his many virtues, and "hard
fate."

About half a mile eastward from Darngaber Castle,
on the lands of Broomelton, near the public road
leading to Stonehouse, stand the ruins of Plotcock
Castle, on a jutting point of the banks of the brawl-
ing rivulet of that name. This fortlet is said to have
been used as a prison by the barons of Cadzow, for
their refractory vassals or prisoners taken in war,
when the feudal chief possessed "the power of pit
and gallows." As it stands at a point where "three
lairds' lands meet," and the glen is clothed with
umbrageous brushwood, and presents rather a gloomy
appearance, popular superstition has tenanted the

ravine with ghosts, witches, and bogles—so that the
wight who has been overtaken in his travels by
nightfall, when passing the place, keeps a sharp out-
look for a sight of some of those aerial beings who
may be "revisiting the glimpses of the moon," and
sporting among the banks and braes around the old
dungeon keep.

The name Plotcock given to this place, is very
suggestive of its being haunted by the agents and
emissaries of the evil one, as it is the old Scotch
name of that being, and is a variation of Pluto, who,
according to heathen mythology, was god of the
infernal regions.

The small estate of Eddlewood lies about a mile
north-west from Quarter Iron Works. Like Darngaber the name of this place smacks of great antiquity,
and carries the mind back to the days of the native
Celtic Chiefs, before the time of Malcolm Canmore,
and the introduction of the feudal system, when
each family or clan enjoyed all the privileges
of freeholders being independent of any superior—
even of the Crown. The word Eddlewood probably
signifies "The freehold, or free possession in the
Wood," and is derived from *Udal*, or *Aedal*, which
according to Dr. Jamieson, is "a term applied to
lands held in uninterrupted succession without any
original charter, and without subjection to feudal
service, or the acknowledgement of any superior.
"The word is much of the same import as the law
Latin term *Allodium*, applied to a free manor, or
independent possession. *Wood*, the other constituent
part of the word, is easily accounted for, as the lands
lay within the bounds of the ancient Caledonian
Forest. But although its possessors, at the time the
name was imposed, were "Udallers," or freeholders,
it seems that before the war of independence they

had become vassals or tendants of the Crown, and
"the tenandry of Adelwood" were included in the
grant of the barony of Cadzow by Bruce to Sir
Walter Hamilton immediately after the battle of
Bannockburn.   This grant is thus narrated by
Hamilton of Wishaw, in his "Description of the
Sheriffdom of Lanark,"—"The precise time when
this lordship was given to the Duke of Hamilton
his predecessors, is not clear; but there is one
charter extant, granted by King Robert Bruce, in
the 7th year of his reign, 1314, to Sir Walter,
son of Sir Gilbert de Hamilton of this barony, and
the tendry of Adelwood, which formerly belonged
to his father, Sir Gilbert, and has without interruption continued in that family ever since." It
thus appears to have been a small barony, and like
other baronial holdings, it had its Castle, Chapel and
Mill.   The Castle of Eddlewood was situated on the
banks of the Meikle burn, within the wall which
surrounds the High Parks of Hamilton.   Its site is
marked by a mound of rubbish and the fragment of
a wall.   The Chapel of Eddlewood stood on a farm
near the present Eddlewood House, still called, "The
Chapel."   It appears to have been built for the
accommodation of the retainers of the Hamilton
family in the upland part of the parish, and was
connected with, and served by an official of the
Collegiate Church of Hamilton.   The only remnant
of it is a fine spring of water called "The Chapel
Well."   Eddlewood seems to have been held in the
natural possession of the Lords of Cadzow along
with that barony, for a considerable length of time;
but latterly a considerable part of it appears to have
been given to a cadet of the family of which little is
known, "A John Hamilton of Eddlewood" appears
in records about 1612.

About the middle of last century it was in the possession of Captain James Gilchrist, a brave and gallant officer of the Royal Navy. He was the son of Mr. Walter Gilchrist, Merchant, Edinburgh, and Grizell Hamilton, the last of the Hamiltons of Neilsland. Captain Gilchrist married Anna, eldest daughter of Major Roberton of Earnock, and had issue two daughters, co-heiresses. After retiring from the navy the Captain resided at Eddlewood, or Annsfield, so named after his lady Anne Roberton. He built the present mansion house, and planted the avenue of beech trees on the west side leading to it, which is said to have been the exact length of the ship he commanded when at sea. The arms of Captain Gilchrist empaled with those of his wife, Anna Roberton are sculptured on a tablet above the front door of the office houses of Eddlewood. These are *Gules*, three cinquefoils, *ermine* for the Hamiltons of Neilsland, of which family the Captain was the representative ; and for the Robertons of Earnock, from which his lady was descended, quarterly 1st, and 4th *Gules*, a close helmet, *argent*, 2d and 3d, a cross crosslet fitcheé, *Gules*. Crest, an anchor, proper. Motto, For Security. The Coat is considerably defaced, and the Motto illegible, but the name Anna Roberton, above the arms is distinct and legible.

Captain Gilchrist's eldest daughter, Grizell, married Mr. Boyes of Wellhall, and after her father's death, got the lower portion of the estate, now called Eddlewood. Anna, his 2d daughter, married, 17th October, 1774, Archibald 9th Earl of Dundonald, and got the upper section, Annsfield and Earnockmuir. She was the mother of 6 sons, the eldest of whom was Thomas, 10th Earl—the famous Lord Dundonald, who was born at Eddlewood House, 14th

Dec., 1775. The room in which he first saw the light is still pointed out. Another son, the Hon. Wm. Erskine Cochrane, was Major in the 15th Dragoons, and served with distinction under Sir John Moore in Spain. After retiring from the army he lived for some time at Eddlewood House and farmed Annsfield, which he inherited from his mother, but latterly sold it to Mr. Dixon, who also purchased at the same time the lower section of Eddlewood. Mr. Dixon resold Eddlewood some time after to Mr. Allan of London, whose heirs are now the proprietors.

QUARTER IRON WORKS.

Proprietors—Colin Dunlop and Company

Individual Partners of the Firm—Colin K. Dunlop, sen.—residence, Garnkirk House, near Glasgow ; George Dunlop, Garnkirk House ; Colin Dunlop, jun. (managing partner)—residence, Oakenshaw House, near Hamilton

Officials—Alex. G. Reid, general manager ; James Galt, manager of furnaces ; James Munro, underground manager; James Shaw, cashier ; Archibald Macdonald, storekeeper

QUARTER LITERARY AND SCIENTIFIC ASSOCIATION.
(Instituted 1867.)

Hugh Jack, president; Alex. G. Reid and Andrew Hamilton, vice-presidents; James Shaw, treasurer ; James Wilson, secretary ; William Rodger and Alexander Bell, librarians — with a large consulting and managing committee

FRIENDLY SOCIETIES.

THE OLD QUARTER COLLIERS' FRIENDLY SOCIETY (Instituted 1799).—Annual contributions, 8s. Aliment for sick members, 6s weekly. Funeral allowance, 30s. John Fleming, preses ; William Johnstone, treasurer; Francis Gilchrist, secretary, with three key masters and four ordinary masters

QUARTER IRON WORKS PERMANENT FRIENDLY SOCIETY (Instituted 1861). Annual contribution, 13s. Sick aliment, 8s weekly. Funeral allowance, £3. The annual dividend to each paid-up member has averaged from 5s to 7s. William Johnstoue, president ; James Shaw, treasurer ; James Young, secretary, with twelve members of committee.

GOOD TEMPLAR LODGES.

OAKENSHAW LODGE, No. 622 (Instituted 1875)

JUVENILE LODGE, "BUDS OF PROMISE," No. 142 (Instituted 1877)'

CRICKET AND FOOTBALL CLUBS.
Instituted 1864 and 1867.

George Moffat, captain ; James Brown, secretary

POST OFFICE—Mrs Rodger, postmistress

Tyson, Thomas, confectioner, London street

Walker, Matthew, manager, Swinhill collieries, Machan cottage
Walker, Mrs, grocer, Wellgate street
Walker, Simon, flesher, Raploch street
Walker, William, flesher, Wellgate street
Walkinshaw, John, boot and shoe maker, Wellgate street
Watson, Gavin, wood merchant, Wellgate street
Watson, James, wood merchant, Wellgate street
Watson, Robert, joiner, East Machan
Watson, Wm., blacksmith, Church street
Watson, Wm., grocer, Union street
Watson & Walker, grocers and spirit merchants, Raploch st.
Watt, John, draper, Argyle house, Union street
Watt, William, farmer, West Machan
White, John, grocer, Wellgate street
White, William, stationer, the cross
Williamson, James, West Highlees farm
Wilson, Andrew, fruiterer and confectioner, Wellgate street
Wilson, James, draper, Raploch street
Wilson, James, saddler, Raploch street
Wilson, John, Raploch hotel, the cross
Wilson, Wm., joiner, 91 Union street
Wilson, John, Highlees farm
Wilson, Dr, Raploch street
Winning, John, grocer, M'Neil street

CHURCHES AND CLERGY.

Established Church, Church Street, ...	Rev. John Crichton
Free Church, Union Street, ...	Rev. William Findlay
United Presbyterian Church, Wellgate Street, ..	Rev. John Shearar
Evangelical Union Church, Muir Street, ...	Rev Robert Brown
Roman Catholic Church, ...	Rev. Paul R. Pies

DALSERF SCHOOL BOARD.

Rev. W. P. Rorison (Chairman), Andrew Spencer, William Sim, Thomas Brown, William Templeton.

LARKHALL SCHOOL BOARD.

William Kirkwood (Chairman), Rev. William Findlay, Rev. John Crichton, Rev. John Shearar, Alexander Frame, John Kirkland, R. G. Cooper, Thomas Duncan, clerk.

SCHOOLS AND TEACHERS.

Glengowan—Master, Alex. M'Knight; Mistress, Miss Jack
Academy—Master, James Brown; Mistress, Euphemia M'Donald; Music Teacher, Jane Smith.
Muir Street—Master, John A. Beattie; Mistress, Janet Galt.
Roman Catholic, St. Mary's—Mistress, Margaret M'Killop.

I—1

DALSERF PAROCHIAL BOARD.

Chairman, Rev. W. P. Rorison; Medical Officer, Dr M'Kenzie; Inspector James Anderson; Collector, John Macfie, Union Bank of Scotland Stonehouse.

SOCIETIES.

BOWLING CLUB.—Green—Raploch Street. President, D. C. Miller; Vice-President, Thomas Duncan; Treas., James Barr; Secy., John A. Beattie.

DALSERF CURLING CLUB.—President, David Frame; Treasurer, James Boyd; Secretary, James Frame.

DALSERF FARMERS' SOCIETY.—Wm. Watt, President; Treasurer and Secretary, Thomas Watson

FREE GARDENERS.—"Thistle Lodge," No. 13. Alex. Gold, R.W.M.; James Hamilton, treasurer; James Grieve, secretary.

FREE MASONS.—"St. Thomas," No. 306. John Nicol, R.W.M.; James Purves, treasurer; John Corbett, secretary.

FREE MASONS.—"Clydesdale" Lodge, No. 551.—Daniel Wright, R.W.M.; James Bryce, Treasurer; James Stewart, Secretary

FREE MINERS.—"Alexander Lodge." Treasurer, M. Gilmour; Secretary, John Potter.

FUNERAL SOCIETY.—Treasurer, Thomas Scott; Secretary, James Downs.

GOOD TEMPLARS.—"Morning Star Lodge," No. 188. William Henderson, D.G.W.C.T.; John Henderson ,W.C.T.; Archibald Barr, Treasurer; D. M'Naughton, Secretary. Meets in Union Hall on Mondays at 8 P.M.

MUTUAL IMPROVEMENT ASSOCIATION—President, John Montgomery; Vice-President, Wm. Burns; Treasurer, John Winning; Secretary, Robert Struthers

ORNITHOLOGICAL SOCIETY.—President, Wm. M'Leod; Treasurer, John White; Secretary, Wm. Burns.

PUBLIC LIBRARY.—45 Union Street. Open Wednesday nights. President, John Corbett; Treasurer, John Ross; Secretary, Robert Struthers; Librarian, Robert Lightbody.

TONIC SOL-FA ASSOCIATION.—Conductor, John Walkinshaw; Treasurer and Secretary, Thomas Walkinshaw.

VICTUALLING SOCIETY.—Stores—Charing Cross and Wellgate Street. John Kirkland, treasurer; J. C. Burns, secretary.

YOUNG MEN'S CHRISTIAN ASSOCIATION.—Hon. President, James Stewart; President, Wm. Kirkland; Vice-President, Wm. Henderson; Treasurer, Edward Currie; Secretary, D. B. Barr.

UNION BANK OF SCOTLAND, Church Street. Agent, William Forrest. Accountant, William Cunninghame.

GAS COMPANY.—Works—Raploch Street. President, James Anderson; Treasurer, David Scott; Manager and Secretary, John Muter.

CALEDONIAN RAILWAY STATION.—Stationmaster, Archd. Beaton.

JAMES KEITH,

Grocer and Wine Merchant,

86 CADZOW STREET,

HAMILTON.

TEAS.

3/2. A blend of Finest Teas imported.
3/. Assam, Moning and Kaisow.
2/10. Strong, well-flavoured Tea.
2/6. Thoroughly sound, sold by many as the Best Tea.
2/. Good Common Tea, free from rank flavour.
1/8. First-rate Value.
3/6. Pure Black Teas, finest selected.

WINES.

All Wines Imported direct and Guaranteed Genuine.

16/.—Tarragona Port.
24/, 30/, 36/.—Pure Oporto Wines, sound, and excellent value.
38/, 42/, 48/.—Fruity, rich flavour and aroma.
54/, 60/.—Tawny, old, silky, and dry.
VINTAGE WINES, 1863, 1868, and 1834.

SHERRIES.

20/, 24/, 30/.—Good, sound Wines.
36/, 38/, 44/.—Excellent Dinner Wines.
42/.—Old East India.
48/.—Fine selected Madeira.
48/ and **54/.**—Dessert Wines.
Manzanilla, Zucco, Marsala.

CLARETS.

14/, 18/, 24/.—Sound light Claret.
36/, 42/, 48/.—Selected Chateaux.
48/ to **96/.**—High-class, old bottled Wines.

WHITE WINES.

Graves, **24/.** Barsac, **36/.** Sauterne, **36/.** Haut Sauterne, **48/** to **60/.**

Carlowitz and Max Gregor Hungarian Wines.

CHAMPAGNES.

36/, 48/.—Sound, fair Wines.
54/.—Ayala.
60/ to 80/.—Ayala, Jules Mumm, Ruinart, Moet, Pommery,
    Heidseick, Clicquot, Roderer.

FINEST OLD WHISKY,

17/, 18/, 20/ per Gal.

J. K. warrants all Whisky at these prices to be entirely free
from patent coffee-still Whisky. They are matured in bond for
years, and have the advantage peculiar to Old Whisky of being
comparatively, if not altogether, free from fusil oil. No new
Whisky whatever is blended with the

TODDY WHISKIES, from **17/** upwards.

BRANDIES, 42/, 48/, 54/, 60/, 78/.

RUM (Old Jamaica).

GIN (Hollands and Old Tom).

HOCKS, LIQUEURS, MINERAL WATERS,

BRITISH WINES,

Bass' and Allsopp's Ale.

REID'S FINEST IMPERIAL PORTER.

GUINNESS' DUBLIN STOUT.

J. K.'s Stock of

GENERAL GROCERIES

Is specially selected for a First-class Family Trade,

And the best quality of everything is sent unless otherwise
ordered. Cheaper Qualities of various Articles, such as Butter,
Flour, &c., always in Stock, and these can be had at prices
much below what is charged for the best article.

Detailed Price Lists sent on application.

SOMMERVILLE & KINNEAR,

Wholesale and Retail

LINEN & WOOLLEN DRAPERS,

Milliners, Dressmakers, Tailors, &c.

14 and 16 CADZOW STREET,

HAMILTON,

(ESTABLISHED 1792),

Announce that they have always on hand a well-assorted Stock of

GENERAL DRAPERY GOODS.

R. C. MACKILL,

CHEMIST AND DRUGGIST,

56 CADZOW STREET, AND 10 BRANDON STREET.

Medicines Supplied of the Finest Quality, and at Moderate Prices.

Prescriptions Dispensed with the Greatest Care, and in the compounding of which nothing but the finest Medicines are used.

HORSE AND CATTLE MEDICINES.

SHEEP DIP, INCLUDING M'DOUGALL'S, COOPER'S, BIGG'S, &c.

WHEAT DRESSING (COOPER'S), and BLUE VITRIOL.

Agent for
Himrod's Celebrated Cure for Asthma—Price, per Box, 4s 6d, or by Post, 4s 8d.
Mrs Seigel's Curative Syrup.
Cochrane's Eye Ointment.
Greer's Pills, &c., &c., &c.

MINERAL WATERS, HUNYADI DE JANCOS, FRIEDRIHSHALL, CARLSBAD, VICHY, &c., &c., &c.

10

WHOLESALE AND RETAIL | IRONMONGERY | FURNISHING AND GENERAL

ESTABLISHMENT,

36 CADZOW STREET, HAMILTON.

ROBERT A. PATON

BEGS most respectfully to call the attention of the Inhabitants of Hamilton and surrounding district, to his large and varied Stock of HOUSE FURNISHING IRONMONGERY, which comprises every requisite in this Department. The following are some of the leading Articles :—

Register Grates, Stoves, Fenders, Fire-Irons, Kitchen Ranges, Hat and Umbrella Stands, Iron Bedsteads, Mangles. Washing and Wringing Machines, Coal Vases and Scoops, Baths, Toilet Sets, Dish Covers, Jacks snd Screens, Plate Warmers, Travelling Boxes, Fish Kettles, Pots, Pans, Kettles, Sauce ahd Stew Pans, Lamps, Gasaliers, Table Cutlery, Nickel Silver, Britannia Metal, and Electro-Plated Goods, &c., &c.

A Large Assortment of

Encaustic Tiles for Hearth and Decorative purposes.

All kinds of JOINERS', CABINETMAKERS', BLACKSMITHS', SHOEMAKERS', and other

MECHANICS' TOOLS AND FURNISHINGS,

Always in Stock.

COLLIERY and other PUBLIC WORKS FURNISHINGS

Of all kinds.

NAILS, SCREWS, BOLTS AND NUTS, WASHERS, PAINTS, OILS, GUAGES AND GLASSES, AUGURS, AXES, SAWS, ANVILS, BELLOWS, FILES, RASPS, &c.

INDIA-RUBBER GOODS of every description

ROOFING, SARKING, and BOILER FELTS.

LAWN-MOWING MACHINES of various makes.

Garden Seats, Rollers, Spades, Shovels,

AND OTHER

AGRICULTURAL & HORTICULTURAL TOOLS.

Fencing Wire, Staples, and Wire Netting.

GARDEN, FLOWER, AND FARM SEEDS.

36 CADZOW STREET, HAMILTON.

Clydesdale College,

(FORMERLY GILBERTFIELD HOUSE SCHOOL)

HAMILTON,

FOR THE

BOARD AND EDUCATION

OF

YOUNG GENTLEMEN

Head Masters:

WILLIAM WOOD,

UNIVERSITY OF EDINBURGH,

(Formerly Ten Years Head English Master, Dollar Institution),

DAVID G. KINMOND, M.A.,

Classical and Mathematical Honours, Aberdeen University,

(Formerly Seven Years Mathematical and Science Master, Dollar Institution; and Four Years Head Master, Londonderry Academical Institution.)

Assisted by an Efficient Staff of Masters—

RESIDENT AND VISITING.

Hamilton Academy.

DRAWING AND PAINTING.

A SELECT CLASS for ADVANCED PUPILS, conducted by Mr R. L. BAIN, Certificated Art Master, meets every *Saturday*, at Eleven o'Clock Forenoon.

FEE—15s per Quarter ; Water-Colour Painting, 21s ; Painting in Oil, 31s 6d.

Arrangements may be made for Private Lessons at the Residence of Pupils.

BELLEVUE ESTABLISHMENT

FOR THE

Board and Education of Young Ladies.

When desired, Pupils are prepared for the University Local Examinations.

All the Candidates of last session obtained Certificates.

Quarter Days—1st September, 15th November, 1st February, 15th April. Pupils charged from date of entrance. Preparatory Classes formed twice a-year.

PROSPECTUSES ON APPLICATION TO MISS NELSON.

Resident Governesses and Visiting Masters.

William Wallace,

CARRIAGE HIRER & FUNERAL UNDERTAKER,

Douglas and Clydesdale Hotel Stables,

HAMILTON.

BRANCH ESTABLISHMENTS—

KING'S ARMS HOTEL STABLES,

HAMILTON:

BRANDON HOTEL STABLES,

MOTHERWELL.

FUNERALS CONDUCTED IN TOWN OR COUNTRY

WITH A STUD OF

BEAUTIFUL BLACK BELGIAN HORSES.

CHARGES STRICTLY MODERATE.

EXCURSION OMNIBUS, &c., &c., ON HIRE.

Coach Office,
3 and 5 Townhead Street,
Hamilton.

UDDINGSTON.

ALLAN CAMERON,

Plumber, Gasfitter, and Bellhanger,

ROYAL BUILDINGS, UDDINGSTON.

EDUCATIONAL INSTITUTE,

ROSEMOUNT, UDDINGSTON.

LADY PRINCIPAL—MISS YOUNG.

HEAD MASTER—{ Mr JOHN CAMPBELL, Formerly of HAMILTON and MADRAS COLLEGE, ST. ANDREWS.

Assisted by Visiting MASTERS and GOVERNESSES.

Miss YOUNG receives a limited number of Boarders, for whom she has excellent accommodation. Children from India or the Colonies may remain during the Vacation.

Board and Education of Young Ladies.

CARLTON HOUSE, UDDINGSTON.

LADY PRINCIPAL, - - - -MISS JOHNSTON.

Assisted by an efficient staff of Experienced Masters and Resident English and Foreign Governesses.

CARLTON HOUSE is a beautiful detached Villa, situated in DOUGLAS GARDENS, the nicest part of the Village, having Hot and Cold Baths, Crouquet Lawn, &c.

The Course of Study embraces;—

ENGLISH, LITERATURE, DRAWING, PAINTING, SCIENCE.
HIGH STANDARD OF MUSIC.
Special Advantages for FRENCH and GERMAN CONVERSATION.

CLASSICS, MATHEMATICS, SCIENCE, and ENGLISH SUBJECTS,	Mr J. PORTEOUS. Mr D. MACRAE, M.A.
ELOCUTION,	Mr W. S. VALLANCE.
FRENCH and GERMAN	Mlle. GIRARDET. Miss JOHNSTON
PIANOFORTE, HARMONIUM, HARMONY, SINGING,	Herr ROTHSTEIN. Miss JOHNSTON and Miss ADAM.
DRAWING and PAINTING,	Mr MONTEITH.
DANCING,	Mr M. THOMSON.
NEEDLE and FANCY WORK,	Miss JOHNSTON and Miss ADAM.

For Prospectuses, and full particulars respecting terms, apply to

MISS JOHNSTON, CARLTON HOUSE,